Profit Marketing
Communications

D1217203

Dear Entrepreneur

Do you know that the average person who starts to write a business plan without the help of a professional almost never completes it?

Your decision to purchase *"My Business Plan Book: New Venture Starter Kit"* has directed you onto a path leading to your success as an entrepreneur. You now have a book that was specifically designed help you avoid those dangerous pitfalls, while helping you start, customized and complete your Business Plan.

To use this book simply follow the step-by-step guide by filling in the blanks, the templates and charts. Each section has been carefully designed to correspond to sections of a structured business plan.

Once you have completed the templates in the Book you'll be ready to write your Executive Summary. It is recommended that you have a financial management consultant such as a Certified Public Accountant, (CPA) or a business plan consultant review the financials of your plan. Next, have your plan professionally typed with the headings presented as they appear on the corresponding pages of the book. Proof read the business plan carefully. Number the pages and provide a table of contents. Package it to suit your presentation goals.

Now you're on your way. Once you have completed "My Business Plan Book" congratulate yourself on your accomplishment of writing your business plan.

If you have any questions regarding your purchase of *My Business Plan Book: New Venture Starter Kit*, send us an email at: info@mybusinessplanbook.com. Also visit us online at www.my businessplanbook.com and www.eprofitmarketing.com.

Sincerely,

L. Edwards

Laurana Edwards,
Business Consultant, Author

1

My Business Plan Book: New Venture Starter Kit

Laurana Edwards

My Business Plan Book: New Venture Starter Kit ^{TM} is a publication produced under direction of Profit Marketing Communications, LLC. Other products and properties include workshops, seminars, and customized materials for entrepreneurial and professional training and development.

Group purchases are available with special pricing

For information visit: www.mybusinessplanbook.com and www.eprofitmarketing.com

If you need the expertise of a business consultant in marketing, management, or a CPA visit our website for more information.

ISBN-13: 978-1467902168

ISBN-10: 1467902160

Dedication

To my daughters, "Toy" and Tanille, who have encouraged me to live my entrepreneurial dream with spirit and passion.

Laurana Edwards

Table of Contents

Introduction

My Business Plan Book: New Venture Starter Kit

Each component mentioned in your table of contents represents a subsidiary plan and, when put together and presented along with the Executive Summary, will become your complete Business Plan. Each subsidiary plan, statement, or description should be written so that if needed, could stand alone to present a specific aspect of your business. For example, if you wanted to put a Mission Statement on your web site you should be able to use the mission statement information from this Business Plan as your source. Or perhaps you want to describe the operational aspects of the business to someone without discussing the financial, marketing, or management functions. The Operational Plan should provide a clear snapshot of the daily business activities that can readily be discussed. Additionally, your Operational Plan should be used to establish and support the system used to operate the daily functions of your business so that you're running and growing the company with ease.

Keep in mind that your Business Plan is a living, working document and should be updated and reviewed to accommodate change. Changes occur with technology, the economy, consumers' interests, the marketplace, and in many areas that relate specifically to your line of business within your industry. As these changes and trends occur it would be advantageous to document change in your Business Plan Book. This approach helps you maintain your focus on the business, while keeping this document current, useful, and fresh.

Banks and private investors become your partners with their money. With the support of a qualified accounting professional, you can use this book to develop your financial projections to support the narrative presentation of your Business Plan. Whether you seek to influence a family member, potential funding partners, banks, or private investors, they need to have a clear idea of how the business is supposed to get started and how it will be managed. You need to know for yourself and be positioned to present to potential stakeholders how much is needed, how the money will be spent, and how the company will generate money from sales in order to produce attractive returns for your investors.

When written with passion, backed by knowledge, and presented as an organized document, your Business Plan will support your dreams of entrepreneurship in ways beyond your imagination. First and foremost, having a business plan takes the guesswork out of starting and running your business. As a result of the work you put into creating this Plan, you will be rewarded with the foresight of knowing what to do next and what to expect. As you create new products, build up your inventory, generate sales, and approach potential investors, your instinct for seizing new and useful opportunities will sharpen.

My Business Plan Book: New Venture Starter Kit is a workbook, written and designed for you to use to create an operational business with ease. Fill in the blanks, use the templates and charts, and generate notes as you go along. The goal is to end up in no time with a completed, well-thought-out plan for launching and operating a successful new venture. Use it! Own it now that you have it!

Here's to Your Unlimited Success!

Defining Each Component

1. **Vision**—*The Vision Statement describes a long-range view of the business. Referring to a specific period in time, ask yourself,* **"Where do I expect the business to be in five years?"** *After five years in business, what do you see your company doing? Do you see a chain of stores? Or do you see an e-commerce business model? Do you see a family-run enterprise with many employees and many loyal customers? Or do you envision something else? Your vision will direct your actions. As long as you know where you want to end up, your business will grow. In some instances the vision may not be very clear. That's OK for now. As your business grows, your vision becomes more focused. You can make changes to your Vision Statement at a later time if you find it necessary to do so.*

2. **Mission**—*The Mission Statement is a statement of philosophy. It represents the principles and ideals established and communicated by the company's leader(s). It is the statement of how you intend to accomplish your goals (as stated in your Vision Statement) based on what you believe in. The Mission Statement speaks of your* **commitment** *and core values as you build relationships with your customers, your employees, within your industry, and throughout the marketplace.*

3. **Business Description**—*As you describe the business, you should include: your company location, the facilities available, and the business's form (meaning, is it a Partnership, an LLC, or a corporation?). Describe whether it is a service business, a manufacturing operation, or a retail business. Include the age of the business or the year the business is expected to start. Briefly discuss the company's size in terms of the number of staff members. Discuss the industry and whether or not there is potential for industry growth.*

4. **Product Description**—*Describe the product's characteristics. Discuss in your Product Description the value of your core product(s), merchandise, or service(s). Expand the Product Description by describing how your product is designed to meet the unfulfilled needs of the consumer. Describe the selling price, the product demand, its unique selling proposition (features), and what is involved with production (if it applies). Talk about trademarks, copyrights, patents, or other related fixtures that add to the product's value and attributes.*

5. **Situation Analysis**—*Create a statement that describes the current position of the business, covering the new venture's assets and resources in a general sense. Present the strengths and weaknesses that may exist in the marketplace and any threats that can potentially affect the business. Also include opportunities that you may view as helpful to your business. ANALYZE THE SITUATION as accurately as possible. If you believe that you do not have enough information to accurately analyze the situation, you can wait until you've done some market research. By then you will have answers to many unanswered questions.*

6. **Business Objective(s)**—*Basically, the Business Objectives are your goals. Ask yourself **"What goals do I have for establishing this business?"** Identify your goals for growth, for marketplace position, client servicing, profitability, or any other goals. Your Business Objectives may involve several business goals or may be identified as one objective. Either way your goals for operating this business are important and must be clearly defined.*

7. **Business Strategy**—*Can you identify the course of action along with the action steps that should be taken in order to accomplish your goals? Sure you can. That's where your Business Strategy comes into the Plan. Take a look at your Business Objective(s). The Business Strategy insightfully describes those key factors that are essential to accomplishing Business Objectives, ultimately generating success for the business. When actively applied, those keys (Business Strategies) will unlock doors, enabling you to accomplish multiple goals.*

8. **Ownership / Management**—*Who are the pilots flying this jet? Who is guiding the company? Who owns the company? Provide a description of the key leaders who will be running the company and describe their positions. Discuss their industry expertise, qualifications, and experience(s). Describe how these relate to the job of leading and running the business. Is there a Board of Directors? If so, list the Board of Directors and their positions. Provide resumes or bios on the leadership team and the owners.*

9. **The Market**—*Remember at least one reason why you're in business. You are in business to fill an unfulfilled need. Ask yourself questions about the Market. Is there a demand for your service, product, or merchandise? What is the marketplace like? What types of consumers do you expect to buy from you? These consumers represent your target market. Who is your key competition? How does your business location help, or does location matter? Are you entering an expanding market, or is the marketplace saturated with competition? Discuss the marketplace and where your company fits*

in. Most likely you'll need to conduct some market research in order to answer questions concerning the Market.

10. **Marketing Plan**—*The Marketing Plan will identify strategies for pricing, getting customers to buy, distributing, and any value-added product features that would boost sales. The Marketing Plan will present the marketing objectives and the strategies that will work in harmony with other marketing activities in order to keep sales flowing. The Marketing Plan tells you how consumers will come to know about your company, its products, its services, and what you intend to do to generate consistent business. The Marketing Plan includes the company's selling tactics, advertising intent, social media gimmicks, product distribution methods, pricing, targeted consumers, use of communication technologies, and any actions planned to outsmart competition.*

11. **Management Plan**—*Who's in charge here? In some cases the owners are not the managers of a small business, and in some cases they are. The Management Plan provides a profile of the manager(s), their skills, business experience, industry knowledge, professional connections, responsibilities, and professional background as it relates to this business. In this section you will discuss the roles of the manager(s). Discuss the staffing required and how management will govern the actions of the staff. Develop an organizational chart if more than one person is expected to run the company and if the company's staffing needs are beyond five staff members.*

12. **Operational Plan**—*This component of your Business Plan tells you how the company is run on a daily basis. Start with performance goals. What do you expect to achieve each day after a typical day's work has been done? The Operational Plan describes the production capacity, processes, and policies set forth by the managers. Whether you're selling merchandise, performing a service, or producing a product, it is to your advantage to create a plan describing the daily routine. Whenever you have day-to-day routine, you have efficiency, which is good for business growth and expansion. Include job descriptions for any work (jobs) that will require staff members. You'll also need job descriptions for work to be outsourced to a firm or work to be done by independent contractors.*

13. **Technology Plan**—*The use of technology is essential in business. Technology produces operational efficiencies that save time, ultimately saving you money. Cost savings occur when less staff is required, and whenever less motion (as in action steps) is applied to performing various tasks. Twenty-first-century businesses must utilize technology in the form of up-to-date software, programmable phone systems, mobile computers, web-based applications, social media connections,*

multimedia communication tools—the list goes on and on, while it all depends upon your budget, your company goals, and the nature of the business. The Technology Plan allows you to describe which technological tools would be useful as staff and management perform operational and marketing functions for the business. How will technology be used when processing orders, managing company finances, searching for prospects, maintaining relationships with existing customers, getting paid, or while performing other duties? Create the Technology component of your Business Plan to describe how technology will make things run smoothly.

14. **Financial Plan**—*The Financial Plan represents the circulatory system (lifeblood) of the business. Often referred to as the company's heartbeat, pulse, and blood flow, the Financial Plan will show you how much financing is needed to get started and how much is needed to do all of those things necessary to run the business without a struggle.*

Equally important are the financial controls that you first establish in order to document profits and losses based on revenue and expenses. The Financial Plan will show you the most profitable options for running the business, while helping you determine what adjustments are necessary to manage the flow of income and expenses. A Financial Plan is essential to growth.

Cover Page

Product or Company Name Here

_____

_____

_____

Your Name _____

Your Title _____

SIC Code(s) _____

NAICS Code(s) _____

Date Prepared _____

Your Company's Contact Information

Company Name _____

Contact Person's Name _____

Address _____

_____

_____

_____

Web Site Address _____

Email Address _____

Telephone _____

Fax _____

Mobile Phone (optional) _____

Confidentiality Statement

The information presented in this Business Plan is strictly confidential and is being provided for review based on the understanding that all written content of this Business Plan will be held in strict confidence. No part of this plan shall be shared with; copied for, or disclosed to third parties without the prior written consent of:

_____

Any concepts, product designs, service ideas, trade secrets, or agreements mentioned in this Business Plan shall be protected by this Statement of Confidentiality.

Or, your version of a confidentiality statement here:

_____

_____

_____

_____

_____

Executive Summary

The Executive Summary is a synopsis of your Business Plan. The Executive Summary should be developed once the Business Plan has been completed. This is important because most of the required information and market research needed to understand the market and the industry is done while developing the Business Plan. The financial projections are prepared as the Business Plan is done. The Executive Summary should summarize as well the financial position of the business. So the Business Plan must be completed first in order to write the Executive Summary.

The Executive Summary should be no more than two to three pages long. If you are requesting a loan or you are seeking funding through investors, you should address the needs of your lenders or investors in the Executive Summary. You should state clearly how much it will take to accomplish what is described in your Business Plan. Discuss how the money will be used and how the funds that are needed will help to turn your new venture into a profitable enterprise. Then state how much you are putting up as a financial investment in your business. Also state how much debt financing (a loan) or equity funding (an investment) is needed in order to give your new venture the total amount of financing needed to start and grow according the Plan.

The Executive Summary is usually read first, and should be positioned at the beginning of the Business Plan. It should summarize the content of the Plan and should be written to describe the key elements of how you intend to establish, run, and grow your business. For example, the Executive Summary should contain information about the owners and their business experience, the key product or service, your intended customers, the industry, and the market. In your writing, express that you have an understanding of the business, the marketplace, and the customers' needs. Explain how the business will grow and how you will ensure that your business will survive when faced with unforeseen challenges.

The Executive Summary is sometimes used as a stand-alone document if it is requested by a potential lender, a partnering owner, or a business investor. So keep that in mind.

Executive Summary

Executive Summary

_____

_____

_____

_____

_____

_____

_____

_____

_____

_____

_____

_____

_____

_____

_____

_____

_____

_____

_____

_____

_____

_____

_____

_____

_____

_____

_____

_____

_____

_____

_____

_____

_____

_____

_____

_____

_____

_____

_____

_____

_____

_____

_____

For an example of an executive summary visit www.eprofitmarketing.com or visit www.mybusinessplanbook.com.

NOTES

_____

_____

_____

_____

_____

_____

_____

_____

_____

_____

Statement of Purpose:

Why are you writing this Business Plan? Describe why it is needed and how it will benefit you and the readers you intend to present it to. If you are seeking funds from investors or from a financial institution, include this information in your Statement of Purpose.

Vision Statement

Your Vision Statement presents insight on where you see the business in the future. What is your vision for this company at the end of a five-year period?

Your vision will direct your actions for operating and growing the business. You just have to know where you want to end up. In some instances the vision for your company in five years may not be so clear. Perhaps you see many things. That is OK for now, because as your business develops and you gain access to more resources, your vision becomes more defined.

Write your Vision Statement in the space provided. Take the time to relax and think about your company and where you see its future. Keep your Vision Statement focused, brief, and to the point. *(Use the sample below as a guide)*

_____

_____

_____

_____

_____

_____

_____

_____

_____

_____

_____

_____

SAMPLE Vision Statement:

The vision for Hillside Property Real Estate is to grow from a one-location, urban-based realtor into a nationwide real estate company with locations in at least six major US cities. We intend to expand within a five-year period, offering services that primarily focus on handling the sales, purchases, and management transactions for commercial real estate.

Mission Statement

The Mission Statement is a statement of philosophy. It represents a long-range principle governing how you expect to run the company. Consider your company's Mission as a series of actions that will allow you to accomplish your visionary goals. What does your company stand for? What are your commitments to providing quality products and delivering notable services? What are your beliefs? Whatever your company stands for should be consistent with your company's vision.

Write your Mission Statement in the space below. Again, it should be well focused and succinct (not lengthy). The Mission Statement should present the philosophy of the company's leader(s). The Mission Statement should not be vague or broad in direction. *(The example below serves as a guide.)*

_____

_____

_____

_____

_____

_____

_____

_____

_____

_____

_____

_____

_____

SAMPLE: Mission Statement:

The XYZ Computer Company services small to mid-sized businesses. Our mission is to deliver the highest level of service to our customers by providing expert maintenance and repair, and outstanding customer service. We are dedicated to becoming one of the leading computer repair businesses in the tri-state area. We value our customers. That's why we guarantee our work.

Business Description

In describing the business you would include the corporate address, the facilities, and the business form (*form* meaning its structure as a partnership, LLC, or corporation). Describe what the business does, whether it is a service business, a production company, a manufacturing outfit, a retail business, or otherwise. Include in your description the start-up year and the business size.

If you need to set up an LLC or any type of corporation, visit: www.eprofitmarketing.com. You'll see the link *"Form a Corporation or and LLC." We can get you started with setting up the legal business form for your company.*

Write your Business Description

_____

_____

_____

_____

_____

_____

_____

_____

_____

_____

_____

_____

_____

_____

_____

_____

_____

_____

Product Description

Describe the product's characteristics. Discuss in your Product Description the value of your core product, merchandise, or service. Expand the Product Description by describing the unfulfilled need, the selling price, the product or service demand, what is involved during the production process (if it applies), and what makes your product or service unique (its unique selling proposition). Write about trademarks, copyrights, patents, or other essentials that relate to the product's value, benefits, or special features.

Write the Product Description

_____

_____

_____

_____

_____

_____

_____

_____

_____

_____

_____

_____

_____

_____

_____

_____

_____

_____

_____

_____

Situation Analysis

Accurately describe any situations that you expect will affect your new business venture. Discuss any resources needed that would give you an advantage. Present existing **strengths, weaknesses,** and any potential **threats** to the business. Also discuss **opportunities**. Take some time to think about your business situation as it relates to what is happening in the marketplace right now. What about the future? Discuss the industry. In the sample presented below, the strengths, weaknesses, opportunities, and threats (SWOT) are characterized as situations pertaining to the marketplace and the industry.

SAMPLE Situation Analysis:

The national cosmetics market generates an estimated $17 billion dollars in sales annually. "Sundae", our new lipstick product line, is expected to be launched in May of 2xxx. We are confident that Sundae will appeal to a broad consumer market. The new lipstick line will offer customers a variety of seven unique shades that differ from any of the shades our key competitors offer. The New York metropolitan cosmetics market is overly saturated with competition, making it extremely challenging to gain a significant marketplace position. There are no barriers to entering this market. We expect to gain a 3 percent market share within the first three years. Through our aggressive sales, marketing tactics and strong marketing budget, we could potentially surpass our 3 percent goal in less than the projected three-year time frame. Long-standing reputations and mass-marketing activities of our competitors pose a threat to any aggressive market penetration goals, which is why we have set attainable goals for market share growth at 3 percent. Internet marketing and social media buzz offer unique opportunities to reach large numbers of customers at a low cost. Both will be included in the marketing plan.

In the sample above, a profile of the marketplace is presented in terms of market size, estimated sales, opportunity for market entry, and competition. Demand is estimated based on consumer appeal. Goals for modest growth are based on competitors' stronghold within the marketplace. In the beginning you may not have enough information. Additional information (obtained from marketing research) is often required in order to begin to write or complete writing the Situation Analysis.

Before writing the Situation Analysis list what you already know about the marketplace and the industry. Describe if you know whether there are barriers to market entry, what marketplace conditions are like, who are key distributors, how much merchandise or service is sold annually in your industry, and what are the requirements to set up the operation. Identify any government-related constraints and list other relevant information. Remember to think of the strengths, weaknesses, business opportunities, and threats (SWOT).

NOTES

_____

_____

_____

_____

_____

_____

_____

_____

_____

_____

_____

Make a list of some marketplace conditions that will require you to obtain additional information.

See the section on Marketing Research for sources of information and research techniques that will help you obtain the information necessary for analyzing market conditions and writing the Situation Analysis.

Market Factors	Strengths	Weaknesses	Opportunities	Threats	Other Situations
Industry Growth Rate					
Barriers to Market Entry					
Industry Size					
Start-up Costs or Business-Related Costs					
Government Requirements					
Market Size					
Marketplace Trends					
Other Market Factors					

Situation Analysis

Business Objective(s)

Your objectives are your goals. You may have several business objectives or you may have just one. Either way your goals that involve the operation of this business are important and must be clearly defined. You most likely have goals for being in business and goals for delivering a service to consumers in exchange for fees. Identify your goals for growth, for establishing marketplace position, for client servicing, and for achieving profitability. Goals should be (whenever possible) measurable so that later on you are able to determine whether or not the goals have been achieved. List and describe only one or two of your most important business goals one at a time. Give your business objectives some thought. As you write down one or two of the most important business objectives, number each one.

Write your Business Objectives (goals)

_____

_____

_____

_____

_____

_____

_____

_____

_____

_____

_____

_____

_____

SAMPLE: Business Objectives

Prior to the official store opening, this company had been selling gifts from home, generating roughly $3,000 monthly in sales. The ABC Gift Shop's <u>primary</u> objective is to achieve 20 percent in sales growth, while operating the gift shop during the first year. Their <u>secondary</u> goal is to open a retail shop inside of the Spring Street Shopper's Mall during their third year in business.

As you can see from this example, both the primary and secondary objectives are measurable.

Business Strategy

I bet you can you chart the action steps that have to be taken in order to accomplish your goals. The Business Strategy statement describes key action steps that will lead to the success of your business. Discussing your Business Strategy does not have to be written as a lengthy discussion, because the Business Plan will provide more strategic insights on how you intend to grow the business. The Business Strategy Statement should be a direct, to-the-point statement, describing an insightfully clever approach to achieving success. *(Refer to the sample below to get started).*

Your Business Strategy

_____

_____

_____

_____

_____

_____

_____

_____

_____

_____

_____

_____

_____

SAMPLE: Business Strategy Statement

*A&G Technologies, a software development company, is entering the business-to-business market of software development. Our Business Strategy is **to partner with major software resellers**. This will enable A&G Technologies to generate direct sales from leads and referrals of companies who may have a definite need for our customized software. When our sales reps contact prospects from the leads and referrals acquired from our reseller partners, we will offer them a discounted software bundle along with a long-term service contract.*

The Business Strategy mentioned here is to develop business partnerships.

Management/Ownership

Who is running the company? Who owns the company? Provide a description of the company's founder(s) whether it's you or more than one person expected to run the organization. Describe the position(s). Discuss the industry expertise, qualifications, and experience of each owner; and how each professional asset relates to the job of leading and running the business. Provide resumes or bios on the owners. Is there a Board of Directors? List the Board of Directors (if applicable). Make a statement on the company's plan for succession (meaning what is planned for continued ownership, sale of the company, or otherwise, if something were to happen to the original founders).

Present Information on the Company's Ownership

_____

_____

_____

_____

_____

_____

_____

_____

_____

_____

_____

_____

_____

_____

_____

_____

_____

BIOGRAPHY

_____
_____
_____
_____
_____
_____
_____
_____
_____
_____
_____
_____

RESUME(s) (*summarized*)

_____
_____
_____
_____
_____
_____
_____
_____
_____
_____
_____
_____
_____

The Market

Market Research

You are in business to fill an unfulfilled need. What do you know about the market? Have you done any research? Think for a moment, then ask yourself. "What information do I need to determine whether the business will succeed?" Discuss the industry and where your company fits. Do you have contacts? Where can you make connections? Is industry credit essential? What is the marketplace like? Is it expanding? Are there barriers to entry? Will I enter a marketplace saturated with competition, or is there enough room to enter this market, earn a truck load of money, and achieve success?

What types of customers do you expect to attract? These consumers, for example, represent your target market. How strong is the demand for your service, product, or merchandise? Who is your key competition? How much will that business location help generate sales? Or does having a prime location matter?

You may already have some information about the market and the consumers you plan to reach. In order to answer questions like these and more, it is important for you to understand the marketplace as well as your industry. One of the best ways to feel confident about running your business is to know as much as you can about the market. To gain more insight about the market and your industry, you'll need to conduct research.

On the following pages of this section, you will be provided with a few key questions that need to be answered before you can define the market. The questions are designed to help you seek the rightful answers by studying consumers, the marketplace, and the industry. You may have additional questions, depending upon the nature of your business. As you seek answers to questions relating to the market, you will also be provided with information on optional research techniques, which offer methods and sources where you can obtain the necessary information. In most cases you'll need to apply more than one technique in order to get the information (data) you need.

Research Techniques

Research Techniques can be **formal** or **informal**. You should select the most convenient and applicable method of getting the information needed to satisfy your questions. Here you will find a few techniques that can be useful in helping you get the information you are seeking. Examples of formal and informal research techniques are as follows:

EXAMPLE
Let's say that the research objective is: **To understand the general interests of business consumers, (as those interests relate to a particular business trade show).** *A research technique of surveying would be* _informal_ *if the researcher stood outside of the convention center where the trade show was held, and struck up conversations with trade show attendees who were leaving the show, and with people who were about to attend the trade show, asking questions and gathering information.*

A more _formal_ *approach reflects a scenario whereby attendees are sent an e-mail questionnaire, or receive a phone survey following their trade show attendance. Or, perhaps once inside the show they are given a questionnaire to complete, requesting a response of their experiences. In these scenarios the formal option offers a structured method for obtaining information while the informal option presents a more relaxed approach to getting the needed information. Both methods have advantages and disadvantages and offer an in-depth approach to conducting marketing research that goes beyond the scope of this New Venture Starter Kit. The important thing to know is that at the end of the day you'll need to apply the most* _convenient_ *means of getting the most* _accurate_ *information needed to better understand your market.*

Observation—Visually observe actions as they actually occur. Observation may be used to observe traffic flow, parking availability, customer traffic patterns, customer service interaction, or any other activity that will allow you to simply look and review. You can use a video camera or take photos to capture events. Observation should be used when you want to obtain a visual / mental picture of events under natural conditions.

Surveys—Surveys may be done by asking questions using an organized printed form, such as a questionnaire, or informally by verbally asking for information. Surveys may be done online, by mail, in person, or over the phone. An example of an informal survey is when straightforward questions are asked verbally, without requiring the respondent to fill out a form (*as mentioned in the example above*).

Focus Group—A free-flowing, informal interview where there is a small group of people engaged in a discussion regarding concepts that relate to your product or service.

Test Marketing—A situation where the actual product is marketed on a small scale under realistic marketing conditions in order to measure sales and determine market potential. Think of test markets in terms of a prototype concept.

Sampling—When small numbers of a population (or a select number of items) are used to represent a total population, group, or a larger number of items. Samples may or may not be randomly selected.

Competitive Analysis—To look at the competition and their marketing practices, while comparing their products, customers, and business activities to yours (or your intent).

Secondary Data—Information previously gathered for another purpose can be used to provide information for your research needs. Secondary data is very useful and can save you lots of time and money. Reading and analyzing reports, articles, statistics, graphs, charts, and other previously organized data offer a convenient method for researchers to obtain information.

Industry Description

Is your industry growing? Is growth stagnant, or declining? For your **Industry Description** you will need to discuss whether or not the industry is saturated with many competitors competing for the few suppliers or distributors that provide services, merchandise, resources, or manufactured products. Or is the industry wide open, with fewer companies competing for the same suppliers and distribution channels, ultimately leading to better credit terms and less marketplace competition? Are there barriers to entering the market, such as high start-up costs or excessive regulatory requirements from government agencies? You need to know if there are trade restrictions, industry certifications, or legal requirements that will affect your business. Are there existing trade networks that you have to become affiliated with in order to do business? Who are the industry leaders? What unwritten rules exist? In order to answer questions like these, you'll need to look at some market factors that could affect your industry, product line, sales, and services.

Apply the **research techniques** below and check the following **sources for information**.

- **Research Technique(s):** Read and review articles and reports related to: your industry, the product line, your services, and the competition. Determine what will drive sales. Whatever affects sales is considered to be a market factor. Learn all you can about market factors and economic trends that relate to your industry and your ability to sell.

- **Source(s) for Information**: Research the industry by seeking information online. Business articles and reports are a good place to start. Look for *white papers* from online sources. Also check related web sites and search engines for recent information that will help you answer the question of whether your industry is growing. Look for news reports on the economy, blogs and discussions on consumer trends, and other sources that offer useful information. Make sure information is up-to-date. Any information more than two and a half years old may no longer be relevant. The more recent the information, the more valid it will be. Contact trade associations and talk to salespeople who work within the industry. After you have done the research, you should be able to provide the Industry Description:

Examples of relevant industry information that new companies might want to know:

- Where can you get the best prices and quality of wholesale merchandise, parts, and equipment?

- Who are the key <u>distributors</u> of your industry? What costs are involved with the distribution of your products? What will it take to establish and maintain distribution channels?

- Who are the key <u>suppliers</u> and industry players? Do their prices, policies, and terms make it convenient for you to do business in this industry?

- How does the online business environment play a role in your industry?

All research done should begin with an objective.

Provide and list the Research Objectives: meaning, what information do you need? Or, what is it that you need to know?

NOTES

_____

_____

_____

_____

_____

_____

_____

_____

Industry Research Objective:

_____

_____

_____

_____

_____

Industry Information

_____

_____

_____

_____

_____

_____

_____

_____

_____

_____

_____

_____

_____

_____

_____

Industry Description

Competitive Analysis

Is the marketplace saturated with competitors, or is it open territory with room for sales growth? In order to answer these questions, you should first define the geographic area in which you plan to operate your business. Check out the competition. How many companies are there operating in your geographic area that do what you do? Identify at least three competitors. Evaluate and compare their business practices, products and services, and their marketing (advertising, sales, and promotional) activities. Also note that because of the Internet, competition has no geographic boundaries in most industries.

Research Technique(s): Observing consumer activity and analyzing reports offer a starting point for gathering information about your competition. Drive around the geographic area where you intend to conduct business to get a picture of the retail mix *(meaning the other businesses in the commercial area)*. It's important to consider the types of stores in the area or along the strip where you intend to do business. Be on the lookout for information on newcomers like grand openings of new competitors entering the neighborhood. Make a note of parking availability and other area conveniences and/or inconveniences. See if you can obtain statistics on business growth in the area and population density—or expected population changes—in surrounding areas. Observe consumer foot traffic and anything else that could potentially affect your sales.

Source(s) for Information: Business libraries have data listings of businesses located in a specific geographic area, which are usually listed by business types. Local city planning and community boards have information on population growth, community development plans, and statistics on the types of companies in the area. Such information is usually organized by zip code.

Competitive Analysis
Use the chart on the following page to identify competitors whose products and services compete with yours. Find out what they offer, their price points, and how they treat customers. Include their strengths and weaknesses. This is important because this is the information that will help you develop the Competitive Analysis.

Competitive Analysis

Competitor	Product Quality	Location	Strengths	Weaknesses

Competitive Analysis

_____

_____

_____

_____

_____

_____

_____

_____

_____

_____

_____

_____

_____

_____

_____

_____

_____

_____

_____

_____

_____

_____

_____

_____

_____

Consumer Profile

Who are your customers? Why did you target them? Are they most likely your product users and buyers? When targeting customers there are three basic marketing concepts to consider: *demographics, psychographics, and geography (also termed* geographics*).* These three marketing concepts enable you to profile consumers as you determine the most effective ways to sell to them. The more you know about your potential customers, the better you are able to communicate to them. From pricing to advertising, communication is essential in selling, as it relates to knowing who your customers are and what motivates them into action. More information will be provided on communication strategies when the Marketing Plan is discussed. Just know that it is essential to have an accurate profile of your consumers.

Most likely you have heard of these terms at some point during the course of establishing your business. For your convenience the consumer profiling terms are presented here with simplistic definitions.

- **Demographics:** The characteristics of consumers, as in age, ethnicity, gender, family size, education, income earning power, religion, culture, and social status.

- **Psychographics:** The lifestyles and emotional attitudes of consumers. Shopping behavior, buying preferences, and attitudes toward a product or brand tell us about the consumers' emotional needs, interests, and lifestyles.

- **Geographics:** Identifies places where customers can be found or where they can find you.

Research Technique(s): Test markets, surveys, and focus groups can provide useful information. By using one or more of these techniques you will be able to profile your consumers. Look at information already available (secondary data) on what targeted consumers need and what they are buying. Observe what is happening in the geographic area in which the business will be established or where you expect most of your sales to come from. Check out the consumers' buying behavior and habits. Observe and analyze transportation patterns and housing markets, which are indicators of marketing opportunities.

Source(s) for Information: Consumer reports, white papers, search engines, and news articles are **secondary data** sources that provide a look at consumer activity, consumer behavioral patterns, and population attitudes. Seek information from local and government-related sources like the United States Census Bureau or local community planning boards. Bear in mind that research data becomes flawed and in some cases useless if the source is not reliable or if it is too old (more than two and a half years old). Be certain that the information you obtain comes from trusted sources.

To gather **primary data,** (meaning firsthand information) you would conduct marketing research using techniques such as: observation, focus group sessions, informal questioning, written or computerized surveys, or any other means that will allow you to obtain fresh information specific to your research objective(s).

CASE SCENARIO

Tasha Sanders wants to open a health and fitness club that will cater to women and men, ages nineteen through forty-five. Her business mission for the health club is to offer a complete menu of fitness services that would promote good health and well-being. She wants to determine the best location for her new venture, because she lives in a suburban area and does not know much about urban communities and commercial districts. She is considering an urban downtown commercial location. At the urban location space is $40 per square foot to lease. At the suburban location space is $25 per square foot. She wants to make a decision on whether the urban or the suburban area is the best location for the business. Market assumptions indicate that the downtown urban location offers higher consumer traffic volume and a stronger brand-building advantage than the suburban location. However, the cost of doing business would be greater due to the higher costs per space and higher insurance costs. Another market assumption is that there are several health clubs in the downtown area within close proximity to one another, meaning heavier competition for a downtown health club. Whereas with the suburban location, it is assumed that there aren't any health clubs within a thirty-mile radius of the surrounding area selected. Her suburban market assumption is that there is a need for a health club in the suburbs so that suburban dwellers will find it convenient to work out and maintain good health.

If you were Tasha Sanders how would you approach researching the geographics?

The first step would be to identify key research objective(s) for each optional location.

- <u>Research objective # 1</u>: Determine the health club competitors; who are they and where are they located?
- <u>Research Objective #2</u>: Determine the health and fitness services offered by the key competitors.
- <u>Research Objective #3</u>: Determine if there is an unfulfilled consumer need for either location.

The next step is to ask yourself some questions on where and how you would get the needed information.

Sources of Information:

1. See yourself as the business owner. What sources would provide information on who your competitors are and the nearby locations of each identified competitor? Well, to start with, online and off-line business directories offer listings of businesses and so does trade organizations. Also, the act of driving around visiting, or just watching (<u>observing</u>) provides a great deal of fresh, firsthand information (primary data).

2. How can this business owner find out what services the competitors offer? Tasha can visit or call competing health clubs and see what they pitch to her as a potential customer. Tasha might even want to work at a health club temporarily to learn more about the membership packages they offer. She could also check their brochures, their ads, and their membership plans to determine what is not being offered; which, as a product or service, gives her a competitive edge if she decides to offer services that are not offered by the competition. If I were Tasha, I would check out the web sites of competitors for a list of what they offer and the locations and geographic areas that are being serviced. Knowing where the customers come from and how the competition treats their customers is important. If you were Tasha, you would also want to find out what social media promotions and marketing programs the competition is doing.

3. Just because there aren't any health and fitness clubs in an area does not mean that one should be there. Also, just because there are existing health clubs in the downtown area does not mean that there is no room for a new one that can offer uniqueness and quality to the area. You will want to know if the competitors' fitness classes are open, or if clients have to wait around to use the fitness machines during peak hour. If you were Tasha, you would want to know if the locker rooms are crowded, and if there are service limitations. Or, you might want to find out if the competitors are struggling to maintain members,

aggressively hawking membership on the streets, in contrast to tastefully promoting the business with coordinated promotional incentive programs.

4.   You will also want to know if a new health and fitness club opened in the downtown area, would you be able to get people to join with little marketing effort, or would attracting new customers be an intense marketing challenge? Would competition be overwhelming? As for the suburbs, Tasha most likely would want to hear from local residents and the residents of neighboring communities about their attitudes toward getting fit and staying in shape. If Tasha established such an enterprise in the suburbs, would it prosper? To obtain this type of information she might use surveys, conduct informal interviews or focus groups, or review reports and statistics on suburban health clubs across the state or the country. As with most research situations, it takes more than one research technique, or the use of more than one source for information, to answer questions about the market, the industry and the consumer.

To summarize the topic on **Sources of Information,** we discussed the importance of knowing <u>what information is needed</u> before seeking information. This is what we call the <u>research objective</u>. Then we placed ourselves in the shoes of potential business owner Tasha Sanders, who had identified her research objectives based on her assumptions of the marketplace, as related to the competition and the consumers' needs. We discussed the sources and uses of primary data and secondary data.

When you start conducting marketing research make sure that you have clearly defined your research objectives, and that you know that the sources you seek information from will provide what you are looking for. Using the information provided on marketing research, you are now equipped to obtain additional information on your business, as needed.

Consumer Profile

Who and Where Are Your Customers? What motivates them to buy? In the table below, generate a profile of your target customers. Relate them to your product or service.

Products/Services	Demographics	Psychographics	Geographic Location

Sample

PRODUCTS	DEMOGRAPHICS	PSYCHOGRAPHICS	Geographics
Gym Memberships	Women and Men Ages 19 - 45	People Concerned About Keeping Fit, Health and Beauty	Local Suburban Residents

Consumer Profile

Provide a description of your target customers. Include geographic, psychographic, and demographic information. *(Where are your primary customers located? What are some of the consumer-related choices made by these people? Present their characteristics as you profile them.)*

Marketplace Demand

Market Demand: Describes the need and want (demand) that customers have for what you are selling. Much of consumers' demand is made up in their minds; stimulated by advertising, publicity, packaging, your prices, and conveniences offered. The consumer has needs that have to be fulfilled and desires to be satisfied. Understanding market demand is the basis for advertising, generating sales, branding, and building loyal customers.

Research Techniques: Some of the research you've already done in order to obtain information on your industry, your customers, and your competitors may also answer questions on marketplace demand. Test marketing is a research technique that will give you an opportunity to check out the buyers' responses to your marketing efforts.

Source(s) for Information: Trade associations and articles on subjects relating to your product or industry will provide more information on marketplace demand.

Research Objective: In this case the objective is to obtain information on the extent of demand for your product, service, or merchandise. Once you have established the research objective on marketplace demand, you will be able to conduct marketing research.

Identify and list research objectives:

_____

_____

_____

_____

_____

_____

_____

_____

_____

_____

Market Research

Using the table indicate research objectives, techniques and information sources.

Research Objectives	Research Techniques	Information Sources

Describe how you intend to fulfill consumers' needs with your products/services.

_____
_____
_____
_____
_____
_____
_____
_____
_____
_____
_____
_____

Discuss any marketplace threats, if they exist (discovered through your marketing research).

_____
_____
_____
_____
_____
_____
_____
_____
_____

Discuss existing and future marketplace opportunities relating to sales and growth.

_____

_____

_____

_____

_____

_____

_____

_____

_____

_____

_____

List industry and marketplace- or industry-related connections you've made as a result of your research.

_____

_____

_____

_____

_____

_____

_____

_____

_____

_____

Market Overview

Based on the research you've done on potential consumers, the competition, the industry and market demand, describe the overall marketplace.

The Marketing Plan

What action steps are you going to take to get your goods and services from your office, your store, your web site, or your home-based business into the hands of your targeted customers? What is the easiest way to make the sale? The Marketing Plan should specify how this will work.

Describe what you will do to get consumers to know about your company. How you'll promote your products and services and motivate people to do business with you is all part of your plan to take your business to the market. In the Marketing Plan, you will identify strategies for getting customers to purchase from your business and to keep sales flowing. The Marketing Plan talks about the pricing, distribution, and coordination of promotional activities and how such activities will function together in order to generate ongoing sales.

Start with the Marketing Objectives (goals). Identify what you expect to accomplish as a result of the marketing tactics outlined in the Marketing Plan.

Objective(s):

Your Marketing Objective(s) should be easily understood and concise.

Marketing Objective(s):

_____

_____

_____

You may have more than one Marketing Objective

_____

_____

_____

_____

EXAMPLE: Marketing Objective—A concise marketing objective for a local printing shop would be: *To increase sales volume by targeting national business customers who need printing work.*

Case of: *The Marketing Mix Mismatch:*

Once upon a time there was a real old-timer named Geo who had opened a jewelry store on a new commercial shopping strip. For the first three years his business grew gradually due to his appealing display of jewelry that was showcased in his store window. Most of his customers lived nearby. But when business slowed down he responded by serving the high school ring jewelry market, which is driven by sales orders from schools.

The merchandise changes made were working for a while, but school orders were seasonal, and he had to hire additional help to sell and fulfill those orders. Then, all of a sudden, when the economy began to slow down business slowed down even more. Geo the Jeweler had to "do something," he thought, and do it quickly in order to pick up his sales. He jumped right in and began selling trophies, medals, and awards, in addition to high school rings. From time to time his customers asked him about watch repair. He responded by repairing watches.

He put a new sign in the window saying "WATCH REPAIR." He neglected to change his window display on a continuous basis. Because he was so involved with handling trophies and awards sales, he was neglectful of the jewelry business. In spite of the big sign above the door that said "Geo's Jewelers," the business looked pretty much like a hardware store from the outside.

In fact Geo sold very little jewelry that year. He was more in the trophy/award/high school ring/watch repair business. Holiday sales were so poor that Geo said to himself, "Starting next year I'm going to advertise more. I'm getting on the radio with an ad that will blow my jewelry sales straight through the roof!"

By the beginning of the following year, some new stores had opened along the commercial strip and one was a jewelry store. This new jewelry store had an appealing window showcase like Geo once had.

One afternoon Geo left the store manager in charge of his jewelry shop while he walked a couple of blocks down to observe his competitor's store. He just could not understand why his advertising did not impact his sales. As he approached his competitor's store, Geo discovered how busy the store was. "Look at what's happening to my jewelry business!" Geo mumbled to himself.

He stopped to question the man and woman leaving the store. He wanted to know why they bought jewelry from his competition and not his store. Both told Geo that they came to the store based on the ad they heard on the radio. *"By any chance,"* Geo asked, *"do you remember the name of the store that you heard advertised on the radio?"*

"Yeah, I think it was called Geo's Jewelers," the man answered.
With a big sigh Geo said to the man, "That's not Geo's. That's not even the right address. Geo's Jeweler's is two blocks south. Did you realize that?"

"Yes," the woman replied. *"We went there, looked in the window. It did not even look like jewelry was sold there. I have no idea what they were selling, which is why we came here."*

Lesson Learned: In his effort to respond to economic conditions and slow sales, Geo lost sight of how to appeal to consumers, the value of his core product, and the scope of his business operation. He needed a marketing plan that would have helped him to think through the steps involved with generating sales, advertising, and introducing new merchandise to his line of fine jewelry. As a result he forgot the importance of maintaining the image of elegance: a quality display and upkeep, which is the norm for the jewelry industry. His advertising and promotions were not well planned. For example, the visual messages were mixed and confusing to customers, as he was trying to promote and sell too many product options. Geo was not a department store. He could have sold the trophies and high school rings using a different approach. Instead he crammed everything all together, resulting in a chaotic approach to doing business.

At first Geo paid little to no attention to his competitor and the competitor's marketing practices. He put no effort into the upkeep of his retail store image. His focus was on sales by any means necessary. The clutter he created was distracting to customers. What could he have done differently in response to weak sales?

Your Notes On Building a Marketing Strategy For GEO's Jewlers

The Marketing Mix: Traditionally the Marketing Mix describes: The **Price**, **Product**, **Place** (location or distribution methods), **Promotion**, and **Positioning** as it relates to putting your business out there. There is value in understanding the Marketing Mix. Outlined here we will discuss each element of the marketing mix and the essentials of marketing synergy.

Price—Let's begin with Pricing. As you develop the Marketing Plan, prices should be strategically set to encourage customers to buy, as you make doing business profitable for yourself. Pricing should take into consideration the competition's prices, the cost of goods sold, and consumer attitudes toward higher or lower prices.

The Product—Although companies sell multiple products and services, most businesses, especially resellers, should focus on marketing their **core** Products (line). If you focus on selling the core Products, it becomes easier to target specific customers. The core Products should be well designed to satisfy customers' practical and emotional needs. Your Products should offer consumers quality, value, and be well packaged (if applicable) so that the Product is protected and attractively presented to the customer. Many other factors are to be considered when products and services are produced and marketed. Product knowledge is a key factor to successful selling. You should know your Products better than anyone else does, especially if it is a product or service that you've designed and created. Consumers feel confident in doing business with you whenever they perceive your products as helpful to them, able to solve their problem(s), or provide a useful solution.

Place—We have all heard the expression *"location, location, location."* Well, the concept of Place in the context of the Marketing Plan relates to anything that makes it more convenient for customers to do business with you. Place may refer to transportation, distribution and fulfillment of orders, location, shipping, and handling. The important thing to know about the concept of Place is that it refers to whatever it takes to make the consumers' buying experience more convenient.

Promotion—Refers to the variety of communication tactics that generate consumer responses that lead to purchases. These include advertising, publicity, sales promotion, product and company branding, and more. Creative promotional tactics may involve social media interaction, special events production, publicity, cross-promotional alliances, good customer service, Internet marketing, and anything that gets your product or your company noticed. Promotional marketing tactics should be well planned with a supportive budget so that promotional activities are ongoing and synergistic.

- Advertising refers to paid forms of media communication that help generate awareness and eventually lead to sales. For example: print ads, radio, TV commercials or online media all charge fees to advertise, based on space, size, and ad placement, as well as time slots.

- Publicity offers a number of options that generate exposure. Publicity does not require payment for space or time like advertising. Although publicity occurs in many different forms, it happens whenever your company gets free exposure that promotes the business. Publicity can occur whenever you make a guest appearance, have an article written about your product, or your company is recognized for doing something for a good cause.

- Sales Promotion offers a direct marketing approach. Handing out brochures, conducting e-mail marketing blitzes, distributing business cards and press kits, or producing a special event all fall into the category of sales promotion. Banners that feature your company's name and logo, hung at a trade show, are also a form of sales promotion. Branding of your product or company's image also promotes sales and may involve any combination of advertising, customer service with a smile, publicity, and / or sales presentation.

Positioning relates to your position in the marketplace. What share of the market can you claim? Market share plays an important role in positioning. Think about ways in which you can establish a significant marketplace position by penetrating the market so that enough customers will come to know about your business among a sea of competitors. It takes a sound marketing strategy and a supportive marketing budget to position your company with a leading edge in the market. Do you have the resources to claim your rightful position in this market? Describe what it will take to establish presence in the market.

The Marketing Mix lets you to create strategies that enable you to promote, sell, and distribute your products to people who want to buy them. One key factor that you should know is that all of the elements of the Marketing Mix must work together. For example, you can have the right prices and the right distribution methods but the wrong product. Or, the right product, the right prices, right location, but have promotion directed to customers who don't need or want the products.

MARKETING MIX NOTES

Pricing

_____

_____

Product

_____

_____

Place (location/distribution)

_____

_____

Promotion

_____

_____

_____

_____

_____

_____

Positioning

_____

_____

_____

_____

_____

Let's Talk About Budget! Yes that's right, the **Budget.** Your company's marketing strategies cannot be carried out without realistic financing. The budget will help you assign a cost to each of the marketing activities outlined in the Marketing Plan.

Start Date	Marketing Activities Phase I	Resources Needed	Duration or Completion Time	Funds Required

Start Date	Marketing Activities Phase II	Resources Needed	Duration or Completion Time	Funds Required

Start Date	Marketing Activities Phase III	Resources Needed	Duration or Completion Time	Funds Required

Social Media Marketing

Social Media, today's twenty-first-century communication medium, is interactive and viral. If used strategically, your Social Media presence can help you exponentially boost consumers' interest in your brand, your products, your services, and your company. Social Media Marketing can help boost sales.

What constitutes Social Media Marketing? Social Media Marketing is the latest form of communication that has captivated the general population worldwide. Social Media is changing so rapidly in scope that it would be impractical to define what it is at the publishing of this Business Plan Guide. The concept of Social Media Marketing is broad. The basis of Social Media Marketing involves establishing a Social Media presence on one or more popular Social Media web sites and making contact with a mass of personal friends, professional colleagues, individuals, professional organizations, corporations, and consumer groups. As interest in Social Media grows, consider learning more. Think of ways in which you can get on board by selectively establishing a Social Media connection or engaging in a Social Media activity. Think of how it will help your business as you make it work for you.

- *Text Messaging*
- *Instant Messaging*
- *Meet Up Groups*
- *Interactive, Online Training Groups*
- *Video Messaging*
- *Face Book Messaging—Friending, Invites, Fan Building, Likes, and Followers*
- *Twitter Followers—Messaging (Tweets)*
- *Linked In— Profiling, Joining Professional Groups, Staff Recruiting*
- *Blogging*
- *RSS Feeds*
- *Skype*
- *YouTube*
- *.....and still there's more*

Companies of all sizes, all industries, marketing a variety of brands, products, and services are now using Social Media to reach new markets and build relationships with massive volumes of consumers. Social Media Marketing is used to move products, promote events, conduct surveys, keep in touch with fans, and do whatever is believed will work. The important thing to remember about Social Media Marketing is that it should coincide with your overall marketing strategy.

It should not be used as a stand-alone marketing tactic. Your marketing plan should also include brochures, your web site, window displays, advertising, special events, cross-promotions as they apply. There is no exact formula or science to this stuff. You just have to creatively look at developing a useful Social Media strategy and include it in the marketing plan. Or you can choose to work with a Social Media Marketing guru. Kick around some ideas on what would make a good strategy for your company.

Bear in mind that you must be consistent in your communication activity once you establish presence and make contacts via Social Media. Why is this important? Because two-way communication online is what is expected, and it's the nature of the Social Media communication game. In Social Media world, the goal is to win friends—lots of friends—and influence lots of people.

EXAMPLE: Social Media in Action

An actual example of a successful Social Media marketing gimmick that's winning fans, influencing shoppers, and moving products among young female tweens to twenty-something-year-olds, goes something like this: *"There are these two young fashionistas who shop for all types of trendy clothing and accessories. After shopping they would videotape the merchandise, item by item, and post the newly taped merchandise along with comments as spokespersons, on YouTube (online). In the video they show the merchandise they've purchased after each shopping spree as they tell the YouTube viewers what's hot and what's not, also letting them know where to get the best shopping deals. So far whatever these two shopaholics say in favor of an item featured on their YouTube post has sold like hotcakes. They have numerous fans who forward their messages to their friends and network on Twitter, Facebook, and other Social Media sites, while sending out mass e-mails to their personal Social Media contacts. The YouTube postings have gone viral.". Just imagine…*

Big companies are already on it. Many larger companies now have Social Media Marketing departments. Major corporations who are now beginning to establish Social Media departments have a demand for specialists and consultants who are creative and experienced in communicating and setting up Social Media connections. Many smaller companies have used and continue to use Social Media Marketing tactics to generate buzz about their products and their events. Social Media Marketing can be used in many ways. For instance, if you want to support a marketing research project, expand your current list of customers through referrals, measure the acceptance or marketing success of a new product launch, distribute samples or invite targeted groups to a special event, Social Media Marketing will work for you. As a word of caution, remember that new media communication should not replace a phone call or a meeting that could close a deal, secure a contac,t or solidify a connection. Social Media definitely has a place in the business world.

To get started you should know who you are targeting, for what purpose (the product and the reason), and you should have other marketing strategies in place. Your Social Media outreach efforts should support other marketing actions. Your goals for executing Social Media campaigns should be clear. To start out, navigate through the most popular Social Media sites before creating your company's fan page. Learn how the Social Media sites function. Think about what you can do to create a successful marketing campaign using Social Media, and how it will work for your company. Follow and review articles on successful Social Media campaigns produced by other companies.

In order to be successful you should dedicate a person to communicating using Social Media on behalf of your company on a daily basis. Also, don't get into the personal chatter or tit-for-tat nonsense of the Social Media world. Keep the content professional and well-focused on your product, your event, your service, or your company.

To Integrate Social Media into Your Marketing Plan:

Campaign for Product/Business (Your offer)	Social Media Goal(s) (The results you expect)	Facebook (How it works using FB)	Twitter (How It works using Twitter)	YouTube or other (What visual images do you want to be viewed ?)

Marketing Strategy

Using information known about the Marketing Mix, develop a strategy for getting your product or service out there into the marketplace. Describe how Price, Product, Place, Promotion, or Positioning are to be strategically used to penetrate the market with your products, generate sales, and succeed. *(In the sample below, the **Product** is the rehabilitation services. **Place** is represented by the transport convenience provided to clients as needed. The **Promotion** targets the medical and legal business communities, citywide, via selling and exhibiting at events.)*

Identify your marketing objective(s) and create a marketing strategy

_____

_____

_____

_____

_____

_____

_____

_____

_____

_____

SAMPLE: Marketing Strategy

*Marketing strategy for the West Side Rehabilitation Center (WSRC) begins with the marketing objective of generating customers from referrals. The strategy involves providing **transport** services to outpatients, and hiring a **sales** team who will go out into the field for the first three years of operation and establish contacts with doctors and attorneys citywide, so that patients and clients are directed to West Side Rehabilitation Center by referrals. To support sales efforts, **promotion** of the services will take place when WSRC participates as an exhibitor in trade conferences and at medical trade shows.*

Your Social Media Marketing Concept Here

_____

_____

_____

_____

_____

_____

_____

_____

_____

_____

_____

_____

_____

_____

_____

_____

_____

_____

_____

_____

_____

_____

_____

_____

_____

_____

_____

_____

_____

The Marketing Plan

Based on existing opportunities, the marketing mix, and your Social Media concepts, describe your plans and strategies for marketing your business, building a brand, and selling your products/services. Integrate the Social Media concepts.

_____
_____
_____
_____
_____
_____
_____
_____
_____
_____
_____
_____
_____
_____
_____
_____
_____
_____
_____
_____
_____
_____
_____
_____
_____
_____
_____
_____
_____

Glossary of Marketing Terms

Account—A term used in the sales profession that relates to the management of a business customer's relationship with the company in order to promote continuous sales and provide ongoing services.

Advertising—A paid form of communication used to promote the sales of products and services by enticing consumers to buy, using creatively influential verbal and visual messages.

Branding—Establishing, among target consumers, product or corporate images that identify a company's product, or the company itself, for the purpose of creating loyal consumers.

Commission—A percentage of the sale, or the principal income value that is paid to an agent for services. Applied most often during the selling process.

Competitive Analysis—Comparison of competitors in the marketplace, by comparing advertising and promotional tactics, pricing, marketplace position, selling methods, product quality, and customer service between your company and other competitors.

Customer Profile—A demographic and psychographic description of customers or consumer groups

Demographics—Consumer characteristics that describe consumers' age, gender, occupation, income-earning range, education, religion, ethnicity, and social class.

Direct Selling—The selling activities that involve the producers who sell directly to the end users. Selling without using distributors (middlemen).

Distributor—A business that buys products or services for the purpose of reselling and delivering them to other businesses, which sometimes involve further resale. A company or person paid to deliver products to retailers.

Distribution Channel—The route products follow in order to get from the manufacturer into the hands of the resellers and even end users. Distribution with the use of organizations and/or individuals (intermediaries).

Entrepreneur—An intellectually innovative person who takes personal risks by introducing new concepts, products, and services to the market in order to exploit business opportunities to succeed.

Franchise—A business establishment that operates based on a pre-established business model, concept, and system of operating principles.

Geographics—Market location, size, and share relative to a geographic area and population clusters.

Inventory—Items purchased by retailers who resell them at mark-up prices in order to cover business expenses and generate profits. Inventory is listed as an asset on the income statement.

Joint Venture—A temporary partnership between two or more businesses or individuals to perform a specific service, conduct a project, or complete a task.

Leads—Contact information and referrals of prospects that lead to sales.

Glossary of Marketing Terms

Market or Marketplace—The arena where potential and real buyers exist, based on the buyers' demands for your goods and services.

Market Demand—The consumers' actual or potential need, interest, or desire for your goods and services.

Market Forecast—Planning of marketing expenditures and returns on expenditures, based on market demand and information acquired from marketing research.

Marketing—Those activities involved with identifying customers, producing products, promoting sales, and delivering the goods to consumers.

Marketing Mix—Price, Products, Promotion, (*distribution*) Place, Positioning, also known as the Four Ps.

Marketing Niche—A clearly defined targeted group of consumers.

Market Research—Activities involved with investigating the market to gather information on consumers' needs, consumer profiles, competitive analysis, and information about the total market.

Market Segmentation—The grouping of potential customers based on their needs, market demand, and special consumer interests.

Market Share—The percentage of sales accomplished by a business within one industry compared to the sales accomplished by its competitors

Marketing Strategies—The strategic insights and expert judgment applied to the marketing actions.

Mass Marketing – Marketing and sales of products across a broad consumer market.

NAICS Code – North American Industry Classification System. A standardized numerical code system which covers trade industries of North America, Canada and Mexico. Often used in doing business with government and corporate entities.

Price Ceiling—The highest amount that a customer pays for a product or service, is based on perceived value.

Product Life Cycle—The life cycle stages that a product undergoes as the product is introduced and sold in the marketplace. Introductory, growth, plateau, and decline are the four stages of the product life cycle.

Product Line—A merchandise grouping of products and/or services that relate to one another.

Product Mix—Related and unrelated product groups sold by a retailer or a wholesaler, or produced by a manufacturer.

Product—A tangible or non-tangible item that satisfies the customer's need.

Profit—Financial earnings gained beyond the break-even point.

Glossary of Marketing Terms

Promotion— – Nonpaid form of communication consisting of activities and messages that encourage goodwill and even generate sales. Promotion encompasses advertising, sales, and publicity.

Psychographics—Profile of customers' lifestyles, personality traits, interests, and buying behavior.

Public Relations—Promotional activities performed by a company for the purposes of generating goodwill and building the company's image.

Sales Plan—A written document that describes the selling goals, actions, tactics, and sales results of an organization. The sales plan is often part of the marketing plan or the business plan.

Sales Potential—The expected share of sales within the marketplace as compared to the competition.

Sales Promotion—Marketing actions, often creatively driven, designed to encourage sales.

SIC Code – Standard Industrial Code – represents a standardized method of classifying industrial/ business activity using a numerical code. SIC usage is being replaced by usage of NAICS Codes. (see NAICS)

Target Marketing—Focusing on marketing to a group of consumers selected based on their consumer profiles.

The Management Plan

Who is running the business? The Management Plan profiles management's skills, experiences, industry knowledge, and professional background. The Management Plan also outlines the professional connections of the manager(s) and their responsibilities. **In this section you will discuss the roles to be handled by the company's manager(s).** Talk about the staffing required. Provide an organizational chart if more than two people are expected to run the company and if you have plans to employ staff. Include resumes of manager(s). If you intend to have consultants work with management, the consultant or consulting firm should be described accordingly.

President/Owner _____

Experience _____

Business-Related Skill(s) _____

_____

_____

_____

Professional Strengths _____

_____

Professional Connections _____

_____

_____

Education _____

_____

_____

_____

Business/Manager's Responsibilities _____

_____

_____

_____

_____

_____

Owner/Partner /Manager
Experience
Business-Related Skill(s)
Professional Strengths
Credentials
Education
Partner's Responsibilities

Financial Manager
Experience
Business-Related Skill(s)
Professional Strengths
Financial Management Credentials
Education
Financial/Manager's Responsibilities

Consultant
Experience
Business-Related Skill(s)
Professional Accomplishments
References
Education
Consultant's Responsibilities

Operations Manager
Experience
Business-Related Skill(s)
Professional Strengths
Areas of Expertise
Education
Operations Manager's Responsibilities

Management Plan

Operational Plan

Can you handle all of the business that can potentially come your way? What is your operational capacity?

Building **operational capacity** will enable you to fulfill unmet market demand(s) with consistency and continuity. The following evaluation is designed to help you establish your operational goals and plan your operational strategy. You do not have to include this evaluation in your Business Plan. Only include the insights that you gain as a result of taking this Operational Planning Evaluation. This is not a test.

With the number 1 as lowest and 5 as highest, rate the strength with which you agree with the statements below:

Business Planning Evaluation

☆ ☆ ☆ ☆ ☆
1   2   3   4   5

1. I know how much financial backing (capital) is needed to launch (or expand) my business.

2. I have a clear understanding of what operational equipment, software, and other technologies are needed to run my business.

3. My company has the essential management resources, such as people with skills and experience, necessary to run this business.

4. I have an understanding of how much cash flow is needed monthly for operating expenses.

5. I know how much staffing is required and the scope of work that has to be performed

6. I know how to create a written system of **policies** and **guidelines** as needed for conducting the daily business operation

1. ____ ____ ____ ____ ____

2. ____ ____ ____ ____ ____

3. ____ ____ ____ ____ ____

4. ____ ____ ____ ____ ____

5. ____ ____ ____ ____ ____

6. ____ ____ ____ ____ ____

The Operational System

Whatever you write in this plan for your business, you'll need a structured SYSTEM for running the business smoothly each day. The work that has to be done by you and your staff should be standardized so that a level of quality is established and consistency in performance, service, and product delivery is achieved on a daily basis. A day in the life of your company should never be a hit-or-miss situation. Once you establish a system for running the business, training your staff is simplified, handling customers' orders becomes routine, and daily operations will function with consistency. Listed are key areas where you will benefit from establishing a system for business operations. The objective is to put this system in a written format so that it becomes company policy. Creating a company handbook, or guidelines for running day-to-day activities, are useful tools for keeping the operations system in place. There are so many things that could possibly go wrong during the course of running the daily operation when there's no system in place. For example, think of that time when you purchased something from a store, and when you went back to make the same purchase you were told something different or even charged a different price. Or, what about the service you pay for that is sometimes on schedule and sometimes not? The prices are not always the same for the same services, either, and suppose the hours of operation are unpredictable? How long do you think these owners will last in business?

Consistency, efficiency, and reliability are important attributes that build trust among customers, which is why the standardized system for operating your business is so important. Create a system for operating your business on a daily basis. As you create the operational system you establish written policies and guidelines for your management and staff to follow. The system should address:

- Hours of operation
- Staff related policies
- Financial record keeping
- Processing customers' orders
- Banking matters
- Ordering from suppliers
- Housekeeping and store upkeep
- Payroll
- Handling customers' complaints
- Producing merchandise
- Customer service

Create Written and Organized Company Policies and Guidelines for the Categories Mentioned.

Establish Your Operational System

Job Tasks	Schedule or How Often?	Skills or Procedures Required	Who will do it? Employee or Outsourced	Work Outcome or Output Expected

Job Description – (For Staffing Purposes)
Job Title
Required Skill(s)
Job Responsibilities
Reporting To:
Educational Requirements
Performance Expectations

Operational Plan

This component of your Business Plan describes how the company is run on a day-to-day basis using an established, functional system. The Operational Plan describes a systematic series of routine activities, policies, and procedures for providing a service, or merchandising and/or producing products. The daily activities involved with running the day-to-day operation should be spelled out in writing. A sound Operational Plan will include job descriptions and guidelines for staff, customer service policies, and procedures for getting the work done. If some tasks are to be handled by other companies or independent contractors (outsourced), you should make sure that your employees know who is to be responsible for that work and how specific activities will function daily in harmony as the work flows.

Describe the work that you expect to get done each week. Consider sales, processing orders, online activities, customer service activities, banking, bookkeeping, and any other required tasks. Effectively communicating through brainstorming, staff training, established guidelines, technological tools, and manuals will create the basis for a standardized operational system.

_____

_____

_____

_____

_____

_____

_____

_____

_____

_____

_____

_____

_____

_____

Technology Plan

The use of technology is essential in business. Technology tools produce operational efficiencies, which will save the company time and money. Cost savings occur when less staff is required as technology is applied to running the company. Businesses utilize technology in the form of software, smart phones, cloud technology mobile computers, and web-based applications. Technology makes it easier to perform such operational tasks as processing orders, managing finances, meeting and keeping track of prospects, banking, and more. How will you use technology in your business? Identify tech tools you'll need and what they will be used for. Attend seminars, webinars, trade events, talk to product representatives and read about updated technology tools that could be helpful to your business.

Financial Plan

The Financial Plan is one of the most essential aspects of the business decision-making process, because economically sound decisions are reliant upon solid financial information. As you start your business, you will need financial statements that are structured based on standardized accounting practices so that the information is understood by anyone who reviews your financial documents. And, of course your Financial Plan must be understood by you as the business owner. To achieve this, it is important that you seek the services and advice of a financial professional right from the start, preferably a Certified Public Accountant, (CPA). The Financial Professional would be instrumental in helping you establish an easy to maintain accounting system as well as assist you with preparation of financial statements.

Equally important to construction of your company's financial plan is the use of financial management software. Financial management software should be used to create the required templates and/or spreadsheets needed to prepare and present the financial picture of the business. Financial software is to be used as a tool to support your financial calculations with a greater level of accuracy.

The Financial Plan should outline how the finances are to be used to **start** the company, **run** business operations on a daily basis, and **grow** the company. Your Financial Plan describes your financial strategy for getting money into the business, and managing the money that flows in as sales are generated; also managing the money that goes out of the business as expenses are paid. All financial aspects of your business are worth describing in detail. However, for practical purposes we'll cover the: 1) The Capital Budget; 2) the Operating Budget; 3) Financial Projections, supported by Financial Statements; and 4) the Break-Even Point. You (and your accountant) can create financial statements to support the financial aspects of planning and managing the finances of your business.

Also critical to the Financial Plan is answering the questions of, *"How is the business being capitalized?"* ***"Where will the money come from?"*** Ideally, businesses are started with sufficient Capital, which may come into your hands as the business owner; through personal savings; or **debt** financing as in loans, credit cards, or other forms of personal or business credit. Other sources of Capital can come from **equity** financing resulting from investments.

Where Can I Go For Money?

The obvious place to go when you want money is…. Well, you know…the bank. Banks are financial institutions in business to make money, as you know. It's important for you to look to the banks beyond your need for money. Your bank should be considered one of your professional associates. You should look to establish a relationship with your bankers. Maintain your accounts in good standing and find out what your bank needs from you in order to build the type of relationship required of a borrower.

Banks, for the most part, hesitate to make loans, especially during a tight economy. Don't let that discourage you, because there are businesses able to borrow from the banks, depending on the nature of the request for financing, the relationships established, and other factors that could influence loan officers or loan committees. You should connect with your banker at the branch level. It's important to know how much you want to borrow and how much the cost is to fulfill the business need for the loan. It is important to know that you are expected to come to the borrowing table with at least a portion of the monetary investment required. Banks want to see that you have financial risks on the line, when you are asking to borrow money. Are you willing to put your money on the table? If you intend to seek funding from a bank loan **here are a few things that commercial lenders generally want from borrowers**:

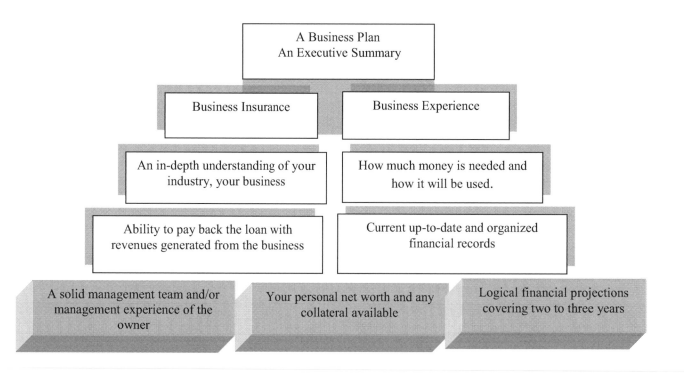

Credit

Trade Credit

Trade financing offers an alternative to traditional bank loans. Trade credit is an agreement to purchase equipment, resale merchandise (inventory) supplies, and services, and pay for those items on account. Simply negotiate for credit with shipping carriers, manufacturers, distributors, and suppliers of anything from inventory for resale, to equipment and office supplies. The objective is to get the best terms, such as low interest rates and convenient due dates, on any accounts payable arrangements made.

Investors

Angel Investors

An angel investor, or angel, is an affluent individual who provides capital for business start-up, usually in exchange for ownership equity. A number of angel investors are angel groups who pool their investment capital so that more capital becomes available to the small start-up business community. Angels are often former entrepreneurs or executives, who may be interested in specific business types, industries, or funding and mentoring entrepreneurs to succeed in business. Angel investors are generally connected through private sources, such as referrals; networking with trusted business sources; and at investor's conferences.

Venture Capital Financing

Venture capital financing is a type of private equity funding provided by venture capitalists to cover early-stage funding required by start-up ventures. Venture capitalists favor high-growth potential companies. Their chief interest is in generating returns based on the company's future value. To appeal to venture capitalists, your business plan must be "investor-focused," meaning that it has to be written to present the business as a strategically sound investment opportunity. Your plan must demonstrate to the potential investor(s) that you and your leadership team are proficient in management, have extensive product knowledge, and that you know the marketplace extremely well.

*The **venture capital funding process** usually involves funding the company in stages. For example, a company who is funded by venture capitalists will be capitalized to cover research and feasibility costs during the "Seed Funding" stage. Once the investors and the entrepreneur know that, based on the feasibility study the business venture is determined to be viable, the venture capitalists proceed to the next round of funding the business. There are generally five funding rounds and in some cases more if circumstances prompt additional funding needs. Funding stages are contingent upon benchmark growth expected by the funders.*

The Funding Stages Are

1. Seed funding stage
2. Start-up stage
3. Second stage
4. Third stage
5. Pre-public or Bridge stage

The Small Business Administration (SBA)

The SBA doesn't directly offer loans to small businesses. The following loan programs are available for small businesses. For more on SBA backed financing visit: www.sba.gov

The 7(a) Loan Program includes financial help for businesses with special requirements. For example, 7(a) Loans are available to aid businesses impacted by NAFTA, for small business exporters, and they offer the Small/ Rural Lender Advantage; an initiative designed to accommodate the unique processing needs of small community/rural-base lenders.

The Microloan Program provides small, short-term loans to small business concerns and certain types of not-for-profit child care centers. The SBA makes funds available through specially designated intermediary lenders, which are nonprofit, community-based organizations with experience in lending, management and technical assistance.

The CDC/504 Loan Program is a long term financing tool designed to encourage economic development within a community, by providing small businesses with long term, fixed rate financing to acquire major fixed assets for expansion or modernization.

The SBA **does not** provide grants for starting and expanding businesses. Some states provide grants for expanding child care centers, creating energy efficient technology and developing marketing campaigns for tourism. These grants are not FREE money and usually require the recipient to match funds or combine the grant with other forms of financing such as a loan. The SBA has the authority to make grants to non-profit and educational organizations in many of its training programs, but **does not** have the authority to make grants to small businesses.

Financial Plan

Think About Your Funding Requirements

Note that funding needs may be seasonal, quarterly, annually or otherwise. The table shown is for

Time period	Start Up	Marketing	Operational	Other	Total
First Year	$	$	$	$	$
Second Year					

planning purposes and should not be included in your business plan

Think About Your Funding Options

Purpose and Uses of Funds	Total Amount Required	Amount You Have Already	Amount Requesting	Funding Sources

Capital Budget—The Capital Budget (see table) offers a cost breakdown of the anticipated purchases of major equipment and technological tools needed to start the business. Such items may include the initial fees associated with a long-term lease, or a building purchase, production equipment, vehicles, leasehold improvements, cash registers, point of sales systems, contracts, or copyright and trademark expenses. Generally, business items that do not have to be purchased over again for at least two to five years (or more) are the items that are listed as Capital Budget items.

Operating Budget—The costs you expect to encounter as the business is managed and functioning on a daily basis are listed in the Operating Budget. The Operating Budget is the reason why cash flow management is so important. You need money to pay salaries, pay insurance, make rent or mortgage payments, buy inventory, advertising, and for other costs that will keep the business up and running. The **costs** listed in your **Projected Cash Flow** statement will itemize the expenses you expect to incur while running the business each day.

Financial Projections —Projections are used to predict how much you expect to earn from sales and other money-making opportunities, and how much you expect to pay out in costs. The Cash Flow Statement and Income Statement templates in this **New Venture Starter Kit** will help you with developing financial projections. With the assistance of an experienced accountant, you can project monthly, quarterly, and annual cash flow (annual recommended for or up to three years) using the formats presented in the sample templates.

Simply start by first projecting the expected financial activity of the company on a month-by-month basis. You can then prepare an outline of the projected cash flow for the full year, followed by a projected financial scenario summarizing a three-year period. Again it is important to seek the assistance of a financial professional who is experienced in working with businesses, especially of your industry. Your projections must allow for fluctuations in sales as sales are generated during future time periods. The company most likely will experience a fluctuation of expenses, resulting from additional marketing, successful business accomplishments, meeting operational goals, and seasonal business activity; also unexpected economic or marketplace trends and challenges. **Your financial projections must reflect the anticipated growth, as described in the narrative portion of your business plan.**

The Break-Even Point—The Break-Even Point is the point where you cover the cost of being in business. It is important to know in advance how much product or service has to be sold, and at what price, is necessary in order to break even. Any earnings generated beyond the value of the Break-Even Point are the company's profits.

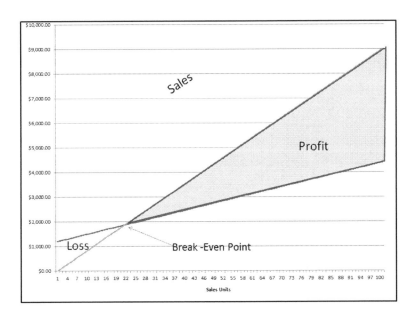

NOTE Your Break Even Goals

Capital Budget

The Capital Budget offers a cost breakdown of the anticipated purchases of major equipment and technological tools needed to start the business. Such items may include the initial fees and costs associated with a lease, purchase of office furniture, production equipment, renovation, vehicles, contracts, copyrights, and trademark expenses. Take the opportunity to list those items needed to set up business operation. These are the items and services you don't have to buy more than once within a short time period (generally two years) to keep the business going.

Item(s) with Brief Description	Expected Useful Life – in Years	Unit Price	Quantity Needed	Total Cost

Operating Budget

You'll need money to pay salaries, maintain insurance, and pay the rent or mortgage. Then there are expenses for overhead, advertising, taxes, and other costs that will keep your business in operation. The statement of cash flow is one way in which you could determine how cash flows into the business and out of the business. Start by listing the sources and uses of funds before creating your Projected Cash Flow Statement. Using the following tables, reflect your estimated expenses, and estimated earnings.

Expense Items	Estimated Costs

Revenues from Sales or Other Means	Estimated Earnings

Financial Projections

The Projected Cash Flow Statement can be created to reflect the projected sales, expenses, and business profitability, based on how much you expect to sell and how much you expect to spend each month. Since this is a start-up venture, the revenues and expenditures must be estimated based on realistic assumptions. (The key word here is realistic.) If sales or expenses peak during seasons, be sure to project seasonal or industry fluctuations. The Projected Cash Flow Statement should record transactions of a sale based on when you expect the money to exchange hands. Some sales are made based on trade agreements (contracts) or credit terms where the payment is expected at another time. The sales transactions should be documented when the money is received by your company. This enables you to project incoming cash with more accuracy. It is not in your best interest to record sales based on the invoice due date or the date that a contract was signed. Payments are sometimes late, overdue, or never paid at all.

When documenting information on your Cash Flow Statement, values represented as a loss or values that have to be subtracted are usually represented in parentheses.

The Cash Flow Statement

How many times have you heard a business owner say *"I can't see where my money goes!"?* It is also likely that you've heard a statement like, *"I know I'm making money but the business is still cash poor."* Consider that a company can be making money, even profitable, yet not have enough cash to pay its bills. This happens to companies of all sizes whenever the company's earnings or assets are not fluid enough to be used as cash when needed. The Cash Flow Statement will show you the amount of cash that flows in and out of the business and the frequency of cash movement. The Cash Flow Statement allows you to see how much cash you have available in the bank (the business) at a given point in time.

So let's get right down to business and start forecasting your company's cash flow. By projecting cash flow activity, you place yourself and your company's financial manager(s) in a better position to plan and budget, as you become prepared for unexpected changes. The Cash Flow Statement provides an important opportunity for financial analysis of your start-up or existing business operation.

The Projected Cash Flow Statement tells your potential lender or investor whether or not the business will be in a strong enough financial position to pay back the money you are seeking to borrow. It also tells a potential investor why you need the funds, and how the funds are to be used over a period of time.

The Cash Flow Projection template (in this New Venture Starter Kit) is designed to help you understand how to create and format a Projected Cash Flow Statement for your company. Again, for best results you should seek the services of a financial professional, preferably a CPA. Financial management software (by Intuit) is available on the Profit Marketing Communications website www.eprofitmarketing.com.

Accounting and Bookkeeping financial management software will help you create the necessary financial statements, templates, forms, and worksheets to manage your accounts and create invoices and other financial documents.

SAMPLE:
Sources and Uses for Cash Flow Projections

Projected Cash In-Flow/ Income	Projected Cash Out-Flow/ Expenses
Cash Sales	Rent
Accounts Receivables *(A/R)* Collected	Utilities
Loan Funds Received	Telephone/Internet
Interest Income	Business Services
Commissions Earned	Payroll/Employee Benefits,
Investment *(Funds invested into the business)*	Commissions Paid Out
	Marketing and Advertising
	Insurance
	Business and/or Consulting Services
	Loan Payments
	Travel/Transportation

Worksheet for listing your Projected Cash Flow income and expense categories

Projected Cash In-Flow/ Income	Projected Cash Out-Flow/ Expenses

Note your revenue sources (ideas and options)

Template for Cash Flow Projections   *Year 20 _____*

Descriptions	January	February	March	April	May	June
Beginning Balance						
Cash (taken in)						
Sales						
Collected A/R						
Commission						
Cash (from other sources)						
Interest Income						
Bank Loan						
Investment						
Sub Total						
Expenses						
Cash (paid out)						
Rent						
Utilities						
Telephone						
Salaries						
Advertising						
Professional Services						
Travel						
Miscellaneous						
Other Cash (paid out)						
Interest Paid						
Loan Payment(s)						
Subtotal						
Ending Balance						

Template for Cash Flow Projections

Year 20 _____

Descriptions	July	August	September	October	November	December	Totals
Beginning Balance							
Cash (taken in)							
Sales							
Collected A/R							
Commission							
Cash (from other sources)							
Interest Income							
Bank Loan							
Investment							
Subtotal							
Expenses							
Cash (paid out)							
Rent							
Utilities							
Telephone							
Salaries							
Advertising							
Professional Services							
Travel							
Miscellaneous							
Other Cash (paid out)							
Interest Paid							
Loan Payment(s)							
Subtotal							
Ending Balance							

The Income Statement

Also known as the Profit & Loss Statement, the Income Statement shows the amount of revenue generated and the expenses paid out during a given period. Income Statements can be created to reflect annual, quarterly, or monthly financial activity. For practical purposes the Income Statement templates shown reflect financial activity, expected to occur on a monthly basis, covering an entire year. The Summary Income Statement will reflect the projected totals for the first year, the second year, and the third year.

The projected Income Statement forecasts future business profitability based on your net sales, the cost of goods sold, and operating expenses. A business can show profitability on the Income Statement yet experience losses or have cash-flow problems. The Income Statement does not reveal the details that reflect how much cash flows in and out of the business, or the timing of cash flow. (*The Cash Flow Statement presents that information.*) The Income Statement reflects revenues (income) once a sale occurs, whether the money is collected right away or at a later time. In the Income Statement, you are able to depreciate business equipment and technology hardware. The Income Statement also allows you to place a value on your inventory. The Income Statement presents a snapshot of the company's profits and losses. Investors and Venture Capitalists review company Income Statements in order to determine profit potential.

Financial Plan

Income Statement Template   Year 20 ____

Income	January	February	March	April	May	June
Sales						
Net Sales						
(Less) Cost of Goods Sold						
Gross Profit						
Expenses						
Salaries						
Fringe Benefits						
Payroll Taxes						
Professional Services						
Rent						
Utilities						
Equipment						
Other Expenses						
Interest (Paid on Loans)						
Depreciation						
Total Expenses						
Net Income *(before taxes)*						
Taxes						
Net income *(after taxes)*						

Income Statement Template 20 __

Income	July	August	September	October	November	December	Totals
Sales							
Net Sales							
(Less) Cost of Goods Sold							
Gross Profit							
Expenses							
Salaries							
Fringe Benefits							
Payroll Taxes							
Professional Services							
Rent							
Utilities							
Equipment							
Other Expenses							
Interest (Paid on Loans)							
Depreciation							
Total Expenses							
Net Income *(before taxes)*							
Taxes							
Net income *(after taxes)*							

Quarterly Income Statement Template   20___

Income	1st Quarter	2nd Quarter	3rd Quarter	4th Quarter	Totals
Sales					
Net Sales					
(Less) Cost of Goods Sold					
Gross Profit					
Expenses					
Salaries					
Fringe Benefits					
Payroll Taxes					
Professional Services					
Rent					
Utilities					
Equipment					
Other Expenses					
Interest *(Paid on Loans)*					
Depreciation					
Total Expenses					
Net Income *(Before Taxes)*					
Taxes					
Net income *(After Taxes)*					

Summary Income Statement   20____

Three Year Projections:	Year 1 20_____	Year 2 20_____	Year 3 20_____
Income			
Sales			
Net Sales			
(Less) Cost of Goods Sold			
Gross Profit			
Expenses			
Professional Services			
Travel			
Technology			
Supplies			
Utilities			
Rent			
Telephone			
Advertising			
Equipment			
Postage and Shipping			
Commissions (Paid)			
Other			
Other Expenses			
Interest Expense			
Depreciation			
Net Income or Net Loss (Before Taxes)			
Taxes (subtract)			
Net Income or Net Loss (After Taxes)			

The Break-Even Point

The Break-Even Point occurs when you have sold enough to recover your company's fixed costs, plus any variable costs associated with the sale of goods and services. When you break even, you haven't made a profit, nor have you experienced any losses. You have only covered your costs associated with selling and being in business. Let's take a look at some of the costs involved with breaking even. One, you must consider your **Fixed Costs,** which are the costs that you can expect to incur on a monthly basis as you operate the business. Fixed costs are those expenses that have to be paid whether you sell one item or one hundred items. They are the costs that include: commercial rent, utilities, operating salaries, fringe benefits, and other reoccurring business expenses that are paid just to keep the business in operation. Fixed costs are also known as overhead costs.

You also have costs that vary during the course of business operation. Some costs fluctuate and are not constant, such as the money used to pay for office supplies, postage, or other administrative expenses. They may occur once, or many times, within the course of a year. As we discuss Break-Even Point, we shall consider such costs as administrative fixed costs along with the expenses associated with business operation.

It is not enough to consider only the costs associated with business operation. You also have to consider costs that are more directly related to the production and sales of your merchandise or performance of your services. Such expenses are identified as the Cost of Goods Sold. *Packaging, inventory, raw production materials, parts, labor associated with production of the products*, or any other costs directly tied to producing the product or creating a valued service are often called **Variable Costs** and are recognized as the Cost of Goods Sold. Almost all product lines have specific expenses related directly to the production and sale of that product.

EXAMPLE

The example shown as *Example F-1* reflects the monthly sales and the monthly costs to produce and sell 100 men's fitness suits of a certain product line for a clothing manufacturer who sells the suits to retailers at the wholesale selling price of $90.00 per suit.

Revenue from Sales	(Selling Price $90.00 x 100)	$9,000.00	*Clothing Manufacturer Example F-1*
Less Variable Costs	(Cost of Goods Sold $32.00 x 100)	(3,200.00)	
Equals the Gross Profit		$5,800.00	

In the *Example F-1,* labor and materials to produce the 100 men's fitness suits total up to the amount of $3,200.00. The Variable Cost is subtracted from the Revenue in order to get the Gross Profit. (See your accountant for preparation and review of your company's actual income statement(s).

Note that production costs may go up or down depending on the cost of labor and materials. Variable Costs associated with production of goods sold can change due to the staffing numbers required to produce merchandise; or the external factors like changes in the economy, which can affect gas prices, wages, or materials costs. Or the owner can decide to produce more or less items in quantity.

In addition to subtracting the (variable) costs to produce the men's fitness suits, the fixed costs also have to be deducted. When you take a look at the manufacturing Example F-1, assume that the fixed cost associated with operating the business is $1,200.00 per month, which covers electricity, commercial space, and insurance. Fixed costs are deducted from the Gross Profit in Example F-2 to show the Net Income.

Revenue from Sales	$9,000.00	*Clothing Manufacturer Example F-2*
Less Variable Costs (Cost of Goods Sold)	(3,200.00)	
Equals the Gross Profit	$5,800.00	
Less Fixed Costs	(1,200.00)	
Net Income	$4,600.00	

In the partial income statements of *Examples F-1 and F-2* you can determine whether the business lost money or earned a profit.

When you break even, you are at the point where you have neither earned a profit nor have you incurred any losses. Now wouldn't you like to know…How much of your product (or service) will you have to sell, and at what price should it be sold, in order to break even?

Let's take a look at *Example F-2*.

Determine the difference between the <u>cost to produce</u> <u>each item</u> and <u>what each item sells for</u>. This is done by simply subtracting. Sales price per item less production cost per item equals the Unit Contribution Margin.

$$\$90 - \$32 = \$58$$

We know from the sample income statement that it costs $32.00 to produce each item sold. We also know from this example that $58.00 of every item sold is available to the business to cover operational expenses (as in fixed costs). In addition, a portion of the $58.00 is profit.

So, let's find out how much has to be sold for the month in order to break even.

In order to determine your break-even quantity and unit costs you will have to use the following projected (or actual) figures:

The <u>selling price</u> for the items or services
The <u>amount it costs you to produce, buy, or provide each service</u>
The <u>operating costs</u> of doing business

Here's what you need:

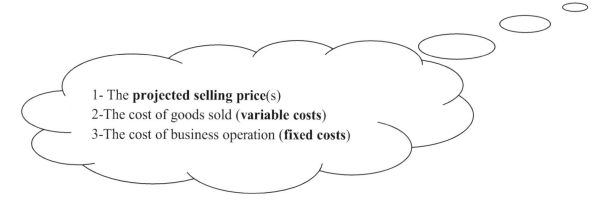

1- The **projected selling price**(s)
2-The cost of goods sold (**variable costs**)
3-The cost of business operation (**fixed costs**)

Your Break Even Formula

P = projected selling price(s)
V = variable costs (cost of goods sold)
F = fixed costs, (operating expenses)

$$\text{Break Even} = (P - V) / F$$
Break Even = (9,000 – 3,200)/1,200
9,000 – 3,200 = 5,800
Break Even = 1200 / 5,800 = 21 items to be sold
21 items @ 90.00 each item = $1,890.00

You can determine the break-even dollar value and quantity for one product line or service type; individually;, or for the total monthly, quarterly, or annual sales.

To find out the Break-Even Point for your company, you can find out by examining your projected income statement to see how much you project as sales and how much you project as costs (as in variable costs and fixed costs).

Step 1 Determine the Break-Even number in quantity

Since you know the selling price per item and you know how much (production) variable costs are for each item sold, determine how many men's fitness suits the company has to sell during the month in order break even. To do this divide the total amount in (operating expenses) fixed costs, which is $1,200.00, into the Unit Contribution Margin, which is $58 dollars per unit. Divide 1,200 into 58 to get 21:

$1,200/58 = 20.689, which is 21 men's fitness suits. Or: $\dfrac{1,200}{58}$ **= 20.689 or 21items**

Because 20.689 is a number close to the value of 21, more so than the number 20, it means that approximately 21 men's fitness suits would have to be sold in order to break even.

Step 2 Determine the Break-Even dollar value in sales

If you know that the selling price per unit is $90.00, we can then multiply the number of items to be sold by the selling price of $90.00 to get the break-even amount as a dollar value.

The Break-Even Point is: 21 items x $90.00 per item = $1,890.00.

The men's suit manufacturer shown in *Examples F-1 and F-2* would break even by the time 21 items were sold, totaling the amount of $1,890.00. Any items produced above 21 fitness suits and any sales achieved beyond $1,890.00 produces a larger contribution toward profit.

Using the decimal (percentage) value to compute the Break-Even Point is helpful when we are working with larger numbers such as annual sales and annual costs.

Using the example above, you can also express $58.00 (the unit contribution margin) as a ratio. Ratios are expressed as either a percentage % or as a decimal number. To get the ratio value, do the following: Divide Unit Cost into the Selling Cost. Divide $58.00 into $90.00.

Unit Cost	**$58**	= **64%** which can also be represented as .64
Selling Price	**$90**	

Here you have the ratio value represented as <u>64%</u> and you also have the ratio shown as a decimal value of <u>.64.</u> This means that 64% of every sales dollar helps to cover the costs of doing business and a portion is profit.

Or, you can compute the ratio value for the total month (the contribution margin) if you express the ratio value of $5,800.00 divided into $9,000.

Gross Profit	**$5,800**	= **64%** which can also be represented as .64
Sales Revenue	**$9,000**	

Do You Have a Projected Income Statement Yet? If you do…

Using the examples given you can figure out the Break-Even Point for your business. If you've done some or all of your financial projections at this stage of your business planning process, refer to the figures presented on your Income Statement. If you have financial statements from the prior year, you can use figures from your last year's income statement. By determining your Break-Even Point, you also gain insight on what will drive profitability for your business. Using a calculator and your Income Statement, you can determine your projected Break-Even revenues.

*Look at your projected **Income Statement** to get the following figures*

Revenue from Projected Sales	$
Less Variable Costs (Cost of Goods Sold)	( )
Gross Profit	$
Less Business Expenses (Fixed Costs)	( )
Net Income	$

In order to project the Break-Even figure for your company, your projected income statement should reflect Revenues, Variable Costs, and Fixed Costs. Note: The Gross Profit is the value of Revenue less Cost of Goods Sold. And Net Income is the value of the Gross Profit less Fixed Costs.

*SAMPLE Projected Annual **Income Statement** for a Service Business*

Revenue from Projected Sales	$ 150,000.00
Less Variable Costs (Cost of Goods Sold)	(23,000.00)
Gross Profit	$ 127,000.00
Less Business Expenses (Fixed Costs)	(45,800.00)
Net Income	$ 81,200.00

Apply the Break-Even Formula

P = projected selling price(s)
V = variable costs (cost of goods sold)
F = fixed costs, (operating expenses)

$$(P - V) / F$$

Using the decimal (percentage) value to compute the Break-Even Point is helpful when we are working with larger numbers such as annual sales and annual costs.

$$\$150,000 - \$23,000 = \$127,000$$

$$\frac{127,000}{150,000} = .85$$

$$\frac{45,800}{.85} = 53,882$$

The sample income statement above shows that the service company's annual variable costs were $23,000.00, which was subtracted from the company's annual revenues to get the gross profit. Then, the gross profit of $127,000.00 was divided into the annual revenue amount of $150,000.00 to get the ratio (percentage) value, which is .85. Next, the annual fixed cost value of $45,800.00 is divided by .85 to get the Break-Even amount of $53,882.00. The company needs to sell $53,882.00 worth of services in order to break even for the year.

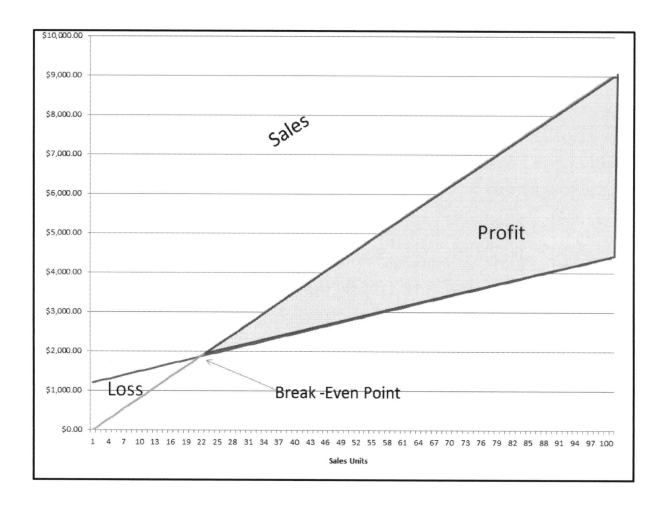

How can you control expenses so that you can break even much sooner than you have projected?

Note: Now that you have a projected Break-Even value, you can also figure out how you can make adjustments in order to improve profitability. For example, just as expected variable costs and sales projections could be adjusted to achieve a more profitable outcome, you can also find ways to project lower fixed costs, since those costs are projected and have not yet occurred.

   a. <u>Sell more</u> merchandise at the same retail prices during that year
   b. Sell the same amount of merchandise at <u>higher retail prices</u>
   c. <u>Sell more</u> merchandise at <u>higher prices</u>
   d. <u>Reduce Variable Costs</u>
   e. Or <u>reduce Variable Costs</u> along with some combination of <u>a, b, or c.</u>

112

The Balance Sheet

The Balance Sheet provides a financial picture of the company at a specified point in time. The Balance Sheet reflects the company's Assets, Liabilities, and Net Worth. The Balance Sheet allows you to present the value of the business by listing what you have as assets, what you owe as Liabilities, and the Owner's Equity of the business. Lenders study the Balance Sheet to determine if the company is in a strong enough position to borrow and repay funds. Investors view the balance sheet for a picture of the company's value in terms of net worth. Suppliers may view the balance sheet in order to see if they should extend credit.

The Balance Sheet will present what the company is worth at a specific point in time. A good financial strategy always involves working with an accountant who will help you prepare the balance sheet for your company. Investors, potential partners, banks, or other future stakeholders rely on the balance sheet to determine the company's financial position, or what the business is worth at the date and time in which the Balance Sheet is being presented. For example, the Balance Sheet will show if the company is profitable, heavily in debt, or, has its assets tied up in inventory or equipment.

The Balance Sheet consists of three parts which are:

Assets, what the company owns

Liabilities, what the company owes

Net Worth or Equity, what the business is worth

To understand how to prepare and review your balance sheet, you may follow the steps as outlined:

Assets

Current Assets, which are those items of value that could be liquidated for cash within a short period of time, are the first to be listed. Cash, inventory, and accounts receivables are classified as Current Assets.

Current Assets are added to get the value of the Total Current Assets.

Long-Term Assets are the items of value that are not readily converted into cash. Long-Term Assets are listed following the subtotal as Current Assets. The list of items defined as Long-Term Assets may include land, buildings, machinery, or other types of valuables owned. If depreciation applies to machinery, computer hardware, or equipment, depreciation is subtracted from the Long-Term Assets. Add up the **Current Assets** and the **Long-Term Assets** in order get the value of the **Total Assets.**

Liabilities are listed secondly

Liabilities are obligations of the business that generally occur as a result of prior business transactions. Some liabilities are short-term and some are long-term. Short-term liabilities are considered Current Liabilities and are generally those debts that have to be paid within a year from the date presented on the balance sheet. Current Liabilities are listed first as the short-term debts due. Current Liabilities may include such debts as accrued payroll, accounts payable, taxes payable, or any interest due. Current Liabilities are added up to get the total value of the Current Liabilities. Long-Term Liabilities are listed following the totaled value of the Current Liabilities. Long-Term Liabilities are deferred tax liabilities or debts incurred based on large purchases such as equipment or the mortgage for a building. Add both the Total Current Liabilities and the Total Long-Term Liabilities to get the Total Liabilities.

Owner's Equity

Owner's Equity of the business comes from cash invested in the business by the business owner(s) and revenues earned from operating the business.

The two sides of the Balance Sheet should be equal. The Total Liabilities and the Owner's Equity together should equal the amount in Total Assets.

The Balance Sheet Equation:

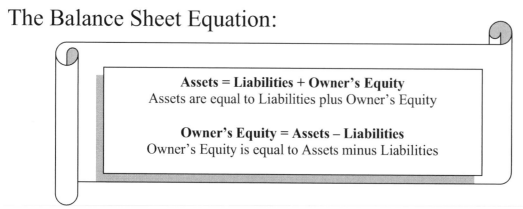

Assets = Liabilities + Owner's Equity
Assets are equal to Liabilities plus Owner's Equity

Owner's Equity = Assets – Liabilities
Owner's Equity is equal to Assets minus Liabilities

The Balance Sheet

Assets		
Current Assets		
Cash		
Inventory		
Accounts Receivable		
Long-Term Assets		
Plant or real estate owned		
Furniture/fixtures		
Equipment/machinery		
Less (depreciation)		
Total Assets		

Liabilities		
Current Liabilities		
Accounts Payable		
Notes Payable		
Taxes Payable		
Accrued Interest		
Debt Due		
Total Current Liabilities		
Long-Term Liabilities		
Long-Term Debt		
Deferred Taxes		
Total Long-Term Liabilities		
Long-Term Loan(s) Payable		
Mortgage Payable		
Owner's Equity / Net Worth		
Total Liabilities & Owner's Equity		

Glossary of Financial Terms

Accounts Payable—Money owed to suppliers for goods or services rendered. Outstanding bills.

Accounts Receivable—Money owed to the business based on the sales of goods and services. Outstanding invoices.

Amortization—Gradual payment of a debt through scheduled payments, or the process of writing off an intangible asset against expenses over the period of its economic useful life.

Assets—Anything that the business owns that has a positive monetary value.

Bad Debt—Debt owed to the business that is either uncollectible or likely to be uncollectible.

Balance Sheet—A financial statement that reflects the assets, liabilities, and net worth of the business on a given day.

Bookkeeping - A system for recording business transactions of financial value. A company may apply either the Double Entry or Single Entry Bookkeeping system.

Break-Even Analysis—A method of determining the exact point at which the business has generated neither a loss or a profit.

Capital—The term used to describe money invested into the business.

Capital Budget—The plan that describes allocation for the purchase of capital items such as equipment, land, or lease.

Cash Basis Accounting—An accounting system where sales and expenses are recorded only when the cash changes hands.

Cash Flow—Charting the sources and uses of funds that enter and leave the business.

Collateral—Assets that the borrower assigns to a lender in order to ensure that a debt would be repaid. If the loan goes into default, the lender assumes possession of the collateralized assets.

Contribution Margin—The total revenue (as shown on the income statement), less the total variable expenses. It may also be expressed as a percentage or decimal value. It is used to help determine how much revenue is needed to break even, profit, or avoid company losses. Contribution Margin can also be expressed per unit sales.

Convertible Loan—A loan made to the business whereby the lender has the option of either repayment of the loan or taking part ownership of the business at a future date.

Cost of Goods Sold—Expenses directly associated with the production and/or making of products and/or services. Items such as materials, direct labor, and freight are classified under Cost of Goods Sold.

Cost of Sale—Costs directly associated with selling a product or service, such as commissions and distributor's fees.

Glossary of Financial Terms

Current Assets—Assets in your possession that can be readily liquidated for cash within a short period of time.

Current Liabilities—Debts that must be paid within a short period of time.

Debt Financing—Loans, and any form of borrowed money, used to finance the business. Once the loan is repaid, the lender is no longer tied to the business, nor does the lender receive any form of ownership.

Depreciation—The wear and tear on fixed assets that allows the business a write off as an expense in value, based upon the assets' decreased useful life.

Equity—Ownership in a company, usually distributed by stock shares. The value of assets minus liabilities. Also known as net worth (*see Balance Sheet*).

Equity Financing—Securing funding for the business from investors in which the investor becomes part owner of the business based on the terms of the investment.

Fiscal Year—A twelve-month calendar term whereby the company's accounting cycle begins and ends.

Fixed Costs—Costs that do not fluctuate whenever sales volumes change. Overhead expenses such as rent, utilities, and salaries.

Franchise—A business that is contractually bound to do business based on an established system of operational controls, business principles, and sales practices.

Goodwill—An intangible asset of value relating to consumers' positive perception of the business and/or the company's practices.

Gross Profit—Net sales or revenues minus the cost of goods sold.

Income Statement—A financial statement that reflects the financial activity of the company's generated revenues and expenses incurred for a designated period. The income statement is based on a standardized accounting method for reflecting business profits and losses, which can show business activity covering monthly, quarterly, or either annual business revenues or expenses.

Joint Venture—A short-term partnership between two or more businesses in order to conduct business.

Leverage—The use of credit to buy a business or major equipment.

Liquidity—Cash that can be generated within a short period of time.

Net Profit—The amount of income the business has earned after the cost of doing business (fixed cost and variable cost) has been deducted. Net Profit can reflect values before taxes or after taxes.

Net Sales—The value of the sale less discounts, returned items, and freight costs.

Glossary of Financial Terms

Net Worth—The value of the business resulting from the company's assets minus its liabilities (*see Balance Sheet*).

Operating Expense—The expenses associated with running the day-to-day operation, such as administrative costs, marketing costs, and technology expenses.

Profit & Loss Statement—(see Income Statement).

Profit Margin—Usually presented in percentage form, the Profit Margin is what is earned after the Cost of Goods Sold and all operating expenses have been subtracted.

Pro Forma—Projection of financial activity. Financial statements based on future or forecasted performance.

Public Offering—The offering of company stock shares to the public, to secure funds via stock sales in the financial market. An Initial Public Offering, **(IPO),** occurs when the company's stock is sold to the public in the stock market for the first time.

Retained Earnings—Net profit after taxes, not paid out in dividends.

Return on Investment—(ROI) Profits earned as a result of investments made.

Revenues—Sales and/or business income.

Securities Exchange Commission, (SEC)—Government regulator chartered to maintain integrity, rules, and order within the stocks and securities exchange industry.

Term Sheet—A proposal by an investor presenting the terms by which they intend to make an investment.

Unit Contribution Margin—The unit selling price less the variable costs per unit.:
Unit Contribution Margin = Sales Price – Cost per Unit. It is used to help determine how many units must be sold in order to break even, profit, or avoid company losses. Also see Contribution Margin.

Variable Costs—Cost that are associated with the sales of goods and services and vary based on production, services rendered, and selling activities.

Variance—An accounting term that describes the difference between what was forecasted as earnings or production and what actually occurred.

Venture Capitalist—An individual or firm who serves as investors, funding new enterprises.

Working Capital—Cash available to the company for the continued operation and marketing of the business. Current assets less Current Liabilities.

Tips for Writing and Using the
"New Venture Starter Kit"

Do's

- *Do write the Executive Summary after you have written the Business Plan.*

- *Do proofread and edit the Business Plan and the Executive Summary so that grammar, spelling. and sentence structure are correct.*

- *Do be sure to use a consistent format where paragraphs and headings are distinctive and typestyles are consistent.*

- *Do use charts and graphs wherever necessary.*

- *Do have someone you trust, who has knowledge about your industry, or someone who is a business professional, proofread the Business Plan after it has been typed, with page numbers included.*

- *Do check to make sure that the financial projections realistically support the marketing activities and the operational aspects outlined in the Plan.*

- *Do make sure that the content written in your Plan is relevant to the interests of potential readers.*

- *Do seek the services and advice of a Certified Public Accountant, or an Accounting Professional, to assist you with creation of your financial statements.*

- *Do keep the Business Plan's page count to approximately thirty-five or fewer typed pages.*

- *Do revise and update this Plan as needed.*

And

Don'ts

- *Don't get too creative with the narrative language of your Business Plan.*

- *Don't over project your financials when creating your Income Projections.*

- *Don't use a small typeface (twelve-point is recommended).*

- *Don't use colored paper.*

- *Don't overuse acronyms or overuse industry jargon.*

- *Don't forget, while writing, who is expected to read the Plan.*

- *Don't forget about this Plan after it has been written. Use it as an active working document and guide.*

My Business Plan Check List

_____Cover Page
_____Table of Contents
_____My Company's Contact Info
_____The Confidentiality Statement
_____Executive Summary
_____ Statement of Purpose
_____ My Company's Vision
_____ Mission Statement
_____ Business Description
_____ Product Description
_____ Situation Analysis
_____ Business Objective
_____ Business Strategy
_____ Ownership Profile
_____ Market Research
_____ Marketing Plan
_____ Management Plan
_____ Operational Plan
_____ Technology Plan
_____ Financial Plan
_____ Financial Statements _(prepared or reviewed by an experience financial professional) The Balance Sheet, The Cash Flow Statements, The Income Statements_

Note that some potential creditors require personal tax statements, credit reports and other personal documents that provide a profile of your financial status.

Notes on Your Business Plan Writing Experience

My Business Plan Notes